GREAT SOURCE

Test Achiever

Mastering Standardized Tests

Grade 5

Test preparation for reading,
language arts, and mathematics

GReaT SouRCe
EDUCATION GROUP
A Houghton Mifflin Company

Some of the materials in *Great Source Test Achiever* were adapted from *Test Alert*, Levels B and C, by Riverside Publishing Company.

Design and production by Publicom, Inc., Acton, Massachusetts

Printed in the United States of America

International Standard Book Number: 0-669-46461-9

9 10 11 12 13 14 15 - HS - 08 07 06 05

URL address: http://www.greatsource.com/

Pretest

READING: Vocabulary

Directions: Find the word that means the same, or almost the same, as the underlined word.

1. a <u>genuine</u> diamond

  Ⓐ precious   Ⓒ valuable

  Ⓑ real   Ⓓ fake

2. <u>purchase</u> a book

  Ⓐ read   Ⓒ write

  Ⓑ borrow   Ⓓ buy

3. a <u>vacant</u> building

  Ⓐ tall   Ⓒ old

  Ⓑ empty   Ⓓ beautiful

4. an <u>injured</u> animal

  Ⓐ trapped   Ⓒ wild

  Ⓑ young   Ⓓ hurt

5. <u>attempt</u> a new trick

  Ⓐ try   Ⓒ repeat

  Ⓑ learn   Ⓓ teach

Directions: Find the word that means the OPPOSITE of the underlined word.

6. <u>admit</u> a mistake

  Ⓐ share

  Ⓑ change

  Ⓒ deny

  Ⓓ fix

7. a <u>sharp</u> edge

  Ⓐ dull

  Ⓑ bright

  Ⓒ hard

  Ⓓ narrow

Directions: Read the two sentences. Find the word that best fits the meaning of **both** sentences.

8. A _____ swam close to our boat.

Remember to _____ the envelope before you mail it.

  Ⓐ fish   Ⓒ seal

  Ⓑ lick   Ⓓ stamp

9. Jane walked to the _____.

Where can I _____ my bike for the winter?

  Ⓐ corner   Ⓒ pack

  Ⓑ store   Ⓓ leave

Go On

Directions: Read the sentences. Choose the word that best completes the meaning of each sentence.

Carla was having trouble seeing things that were far away. She had to __(10)__ in order to see the blackboard. Carla made an __(11)__ with the doctor to have her eyes checked. Then she circled the date on her __(12)__ so she wouldn't forget.

10. (A) squint

(B) blink

(C) pretend

(D) gaze

11. (A) invitation

(B) exchange

(C) appointment

(D) excuse

12. (A) watch

(B) message

(C) letter

(D) calendar

Directions: Choose the word or phrase that gives the meaning of the underlined prefix or suffix.

13. <u>sub</u>marine   <u>sub</u>way

(A) after

(B) under

(C) before

(D) in a state of

14. <u>dis</u>honest   <u>dis</u>trustful

(A) before

(B) wrongly

(C) filled with

(D) opposite

15. child<u>ish</u>   sheep<u>ish</u>

(A) against

(B) one who

(C) of or like

(D) without

Directions: Read the sentence and the question. Find the word that best answers the question.

16. Melinda received a _____ gift from Jesse.

Which word suggests that the gift was special?

(A) unique

(B) decent

(C) lovely

(D) fragile

17. Vincent wrote a _____ story.

Which word suggests that the story was funny?

(A) ridiculous

(B) childish

(C) delightful

(D) humorous

Stop

READING: Comprehension

Directions: Read each passage. Choose the best answer to each question.

What is a decathlon?

A decathlon is an athletic contest that consists of ten different track and field events, such as the high jump and discus throw. Athletes compete in all ten events over two days. The winner of the decathlon is considered to be the best in the world at running, jumping, and throwing. That person is often called the "World's Greatest Athlete."

An American, Dan O'Brien, won the gold medal in the decathlon at the 1996 Summer Olympics. He believes that to be a good "decathlete," you need to be a good loser. You can't expect to be great all the time in all ten events. If he doesn't do well in one event, he tries to put that behind him before competing in the next event. By learning to become a good loser, Dan O'Brien also learned how to become a great winner. In 1996, people called him the World's Greatest Athlete.

---

18. A decathlon involves ten different events in –

   Ⓐ team sports

   Ⓑ swimming

   Ⓒ track and field

   Ⓓ winter sports

19. A good title for this passage would be –

   Ⓐ "How to Win the Decathlon"

   Ⓑ "The Summer Olympics"

   Ⓒ "The World's Greatest Athletes"

   Ⓓ "The Life of Dan O'Brien"

20. This passage is most like a –

   Ⓐ myth

   Ⓑ fairy tale

   Ⓒ mystery

   Ⓓ magazine article

21. Which statement is an opinion?

   Ⓐ Athletes compete in all ten events.

   Ⓑ A decathlon takes two days.

   Ⓒ A decathlon is an athletic contest.

   Ⓓ To be a good decathlete, you need to be a good loser.

No Pass, No Sports

Dear Editor:

This year Montvale Middle School has a "no pass, no sports" rule. This rule says that to play on a school sports team, kids at our school have to pass all their classes. My friends and I think this rule is unfair. We all know some kids who are good at sports but have trouble learning. Maybe some will drop out of school if they can't play sports.

Someone told me that he read somewhere that kids who play sports feel better about themselves. They are more <u>confident</u> at school. Sports are good for kids!

Right now, some kids can't play on our soccer team because they are not passing one of their classes. One of them was our star player last year. Without him, our team will be up a creek without a paddle! Everyone thinks Marshall should be allowed to play. Maybe if enough people call or write to our school about it, they'll change the rule. So, call or write today. Our soccer team needs your help!

Juan Ramos

---

22. This letter was written by a —

(A) parent
(B) student
(C) teacher
(D) coach

23. The letter says, "They are more <u>confident</u> at school." <u>Confident</u> means —

(A) shy
(B) smart
(C) afraid
(D) sure

24. "Our team will be up a creek without a paddle" means that —

(A) the players will take a canoe trip
(B) the team will not do well
(C) the team will lose its equipment
(D) all the players will quit

25. Juan wrote this letter mainly to —

(A) express concern for kids who are dropping out of school
(B) show support for the "no pass, no sports" rule
(C) try to get Marshall back on the soccer team
(D) let people know what is going on at Montvale Middle School

26. Juan's letter would have been more convincing if he had —

(A) given facts to support his beliefs
(B) used humor to make it friendlier
(C) added more statements about what everyone else thinks
(D) included the names of all the players on the soccer team

Go On

What happened at Julia's birthday party?

Marcy planned a surprise birthday party for her friend, Julia. Then she called four of Julia's friends and invited them over to her house on Friday night. They all arrived before Julia did, just as Marcy had planned. When Julia knocked on the door, everyone ran and hid in Marcy's bedroom.

Julia had barely sat down on Marcy's bed when everyone suddenly jumped out and yelled, "Surprise!" Julia almost fell off the bed. Within minutes, she was surrounded by girls screaming "Happy Birthday!" Julia's mouth dropped open. She didn't know what to say. Finally she looked at Marcy and said, "Gosh, Marcy, I don't know how to tell you this, but . . . it's not my birthday."

It was Marcy's turn to be surprised.

---

27. What happens first in this story?

   Ⓐ Julia tells Marcy it isn't her birthday.

   Ⓑ Marcy plans a surprise birthday party for Julia.

   Ⓒ Everyone jumps out and yells, "Surprise!"

   Ⓓ Marcy invites Julia's friends to a surprise party.

28. Where does this story take place?

   Ⓐ in Julia's bedroom

   Ⓑ at the girls' school

   Ⓒ at Marcy's house

   Ⓓ in a hotel room

29. Julia's friends hid in the bedroom because they —

   Ⓐ wanted to surprise her

   Ⓑ did not want to see her

   Ⓒ knew it was not her birthday

   Ⓓ did not bring any gifts for her

30. What can you conclude about Marcy from reading this story?

   Ⓐ She always plans ahead.

   Ⓑ She is a thoughtful person.

   Ⓒ She likes to fool people.

   Ⓓ She is a selfish person.

31. Which is the best title for this story?

   Ⓐ "Planning a Party"

   Ⓑ "Julia and Her Friends"

   Ⓒ "The Perfect Present"

   Ⓓ "Marcy's Surprise"

32. How did Marcy probably feel when Julia told her it was not her birthday?

   Ⓐ delighted

   Ⓑ embarrassed

   Ⓒ resentful

   Ⓓ suspicious

Go On →

Guilty . . . Until Proven Innocent

The animals all heard Ostrich screech and came running as fast as they could. They all stopped when they saw Ostrich. She was running frantically in circles, her long thin legs kicking up small clouds of dust behind her. "Ostrich, what's the matter?" they asked.

"Hyena stole my eggs," she screeched. "They were right here in the sand, and now they're gone," she moaned. Just then one of the animals spotted Hyena over by the water hole.

"There he is!" he cried. The animals ran down to the water hole and surrounded Hyena.

"What's going on?" asked Hyena, laughing nervously.

"I turned my back for one minute, and you stole my eggs," accused Ostrich. "I came down for a quick drink of water, and when I went back, my eggs were gone." She pointed in the opposite direction from which they had all come.

"You mean that way, don't you?" said one of the animals, pointing the other way. Ostrich looked confused for a moment, then she took off running in the direction she had just pointed.

"They're here!" she cried. "My eggs are here! Oh, I feel so foolish," she said. Then she buried her head in the sand.

33. What was Ostrich's problem?

(A) She couldn't stop running in circles.

(B) Her head was stuck in the sand.

(C) She couldn't find her eggs.

(D) Her legs were long and thin.

34. What will probably happen next in this story?

(A) Hyena will steal Ostrich's eggs.

(B) Ostrich will apologize to Hyena.

(C) The animals will punish Hyena.

(D) Ostrich will go get a drink of water.

35. How is Hyena different from the other animals?

(A) He doesn't come running to see what is the matter with Ostrich.

(B) He kicks up small clouds of dust when he runs.

(C) He is good friends with Ostrich.

(D) He is a thief and can't be trusted.

36. The theme of this story is mostly concerned with —

(A) judging others by their appearance

(B) making fun of others

(C) helping one's neighbors

(D) blaming others for your mistakes

Pretest

LANGUAGE ARTS: Mechanics and Usage

Directions: Read each sentence and look at the underlined word or words. Look for a mistake in capitalization, punctuation, or word usage. If you find a mistake, choose the best way to write the underlined part of the sentence. If there is no mistake, fill in the bubble beside answer D, "Correct as is."

1. The finish is the <u>most hardest</u> part of the race.

   Ⓐ most hard

   Ⓑ most harder

   Ⓒ hardest

   Ⓓ Correct as is

2. Craig <u>bringed</u> his books home.

   Ⓐ brought

   Ⓑ brang

   Ⓒ branged

   Ⓓ Correct as is

3. She said, <u>Your wish is my command."</u>

   Ⓐ "Your wish is my command.

   Ⓑ "Your wish is my command."

   Ⓒ Your wish is my command.

   Ⓓ Correct as is

4. Why are you wearing <u>Paul's</u> shirt?

   Ⓐ Pauls

   Ⓑ Pauls'

   Ⓒ Paul's'

   Ⓓ Correct as is

5. I <u>hardly never</u> eat lunch at school.

   Ⓐ hardly don't never

   Ⓑ hardly ever

   Ⓒ hardly don't ever

   Ⓓ Correct as is

6. <u>Barbara P Holmes</u> is an author.

   Ⓐ Barbara P. Holmes

   Ⓑ Barbara. P. Holmes

   Ⓒ Barbara P. Holmes.

   Ⓓ Correct as is

7. <u>She and me</u> are in the school play.

   Ⓐ Her and me

   Ⓑ Me and she

   Ⓒ She and I

   Ⓓ Correct as is

8. Our class is reading a book called *The Wind in the Willows*.

   Ⓐ *The Wind In The Willows*

   Ⓑ *the Wind in the Willows*

   Ⓒ *The wind in the willows*

   Ⓓ Correct as is

9. These tomatoes <u>isn't</u> ripe yet.

   Ⓐ aren't

   Ⓑ is not

   Ⓒ ain't

   Ⓓ Correct as is

Go On →

Directions: Read the sentences and look at the underlined words. Find the underlined word that has a mistake in spelling. If there are no mistakes in spelling, fill in the bubble beside answer D, "No mistake."

10. Ⓐ John lost his <u>balance</u>.
   Ⓑ He fell on the <u>pavement</u>.
   Ⓒ Now he has a <u>bruize</u> on his arm.
   Ⓓ No mistake

11. Ⓐ Our class held an <u>election</u>.
   Ⓑ The <u>principle</u> counted the votes.
   Ⓒ He will <u>announce</u> the winner soon.
   Ⓓ No mistake

12. Ⓐ I love <u>classical</u> music.
   Ⓑ My favorite <u>composer</u> is Mozart.
   Ⓒ I'd love to read his <u>biography</u>.
   Ⓓ No mistake

13. Ⓐ Sweets are <u>forbiden</u> before dinner.
   Ⓑ The children can't wait for <u>dessert</u>.
   Ⓒ First, they must eat their <u>vegetables</u>.
   Ⓓ No mistake

14. Ⓐ Troy received his <u>allowance</u> today.
   Ⓑ He made a <u>deposite</u> at the bank.
   Ⓒ Now he can <u>afford</u> new skates.
   Ⓓ No mistake

15. Ⓐ Tess writes daily in her <u>dairy</u>.
   Ⓑ She enjoys writing in her <u>journal</u>.
   Ⓒ She covers a <u>variety</u> of topics.
   Ⓓ No mistake

Directions: Find the answer that is a complete sentence written correctly.

16. Ⓐ Too many pumpkins in the garden.
   Ⓑ Choosing the biggest one.
   Ⓒ Carving it with a knife.
   Ⓓ Pumpkin seeds are good to eat.

17. Ⓐ Loves to cook for his friends.
   Ⓑ Jeff's dad was a chef.
   Ⓒ Always calling him for recipes.
   Ⓓ Last night, the best meal ever.

18. Ⓐ Was once an orphan.
   Ⓑ Adopted by kind people.
   Ⓒ Manny has two wonderful parents.
   Ⓓ Often visits other orphans.

19. Ⓐ Josh hasn't done his homework yet.
   Ⓑ Putting off reading until later.
   Ⓒ Books forgotten at school.
   Ⓓ About to start math homework.

20. Ⓐ Kim forgot her lunch she left it on the kitchen counter.
   Ⓑ She phoned her mom and asked her to bring her lunch to school.
   Ⓒ Waiting patiently in the hall.
   Ⓓ Brought Kim's lunch to school.

21. Ⓐ Choosing science projects.
   Ⓑ They split up into groups each picked a different project.
   Ⓒ So many interesting projects to choose from.
   Ⓓ Everyone finished their projects in time for the science fair.

Stop

Pretest

LANGUAGE ARTS: Composition

Directions: Read each paragraph. Then answer the questions that follow.

Paragraph 1

Our shoes can give other people clues about what we like to do. For example, ballet dancers wear ballet slippers, soccer players wear cleats, and runners wear running shoes. The first shoes were made over one thousand years ago. Our shoes also tell something about our personalities. They may tell others that we are active. They may tell others that we are stylish.

---

22. Which is the best topic sentence for this paragraph?

Ⓐ When is the last time you bought a new pair of shoes?

Ⓑ People can tell a lot about us by the shoes we wear.

Ⓒ Shoes come in many different sizes and styles.

Ⓓ Old shoes should be thrown away.

23. Which is the best way to combine the last two sentences in this paragraph?

Ⓐ They may tell others that we are active or stylish.

Ⓑ They may tell others that we are active but not stylish.

Ⓒ They may tell others that we are stylish but also active.

Ⓓ They may tell others that we are active rather than stylish.

24. Which sentence would fit best at the end of this paragraph?

Ⓐ Go out and buy yourself a new pair of shoes today!

Ⓑ A comfortable pair of shoes can change a person's life.

Ⓒ To fool people into thinking you are a cowboy, wear cowboy boots.

Ⓓ What do your shoes say about you?

25. Which sentence does **not** belong in this paragraph?

Ⓐ Our shoes also tell something about our personalities.

Ⓑ Our shoes can give other people clues about what we like to do.

Ⓒ The first shoes were made over one thousand years ago.

Ⓓ They may tell others that we are active.

Go On →

Paragraph 2

First, make sure your dog is on a leash. Let your dog walk around for a while. Then say the dog's name and "Come!" Tug on the leash gently to pull the dog toward you. If your dog doesn't come, repeat the command while gently tugging on the leash. Praise your dog when it obeys. Never scold your dog if it does not come right away. Never punish your dog if it does not come right away.

---

26. Which is the best topic sentence for this paragraph?

Ⓐ Dogs are man's best friend.

Ⓑ Here are some simple tips for teaching your dog to come when you call.

Ⓒ Teaching a dog new tricks can be fun!

Ⓓ If you're lucky, you can sometimes get a great dog at the pound.

27. Which is the best way to combine the last two sentences in this paragraph?

Ⓐ Never scold or never punish your dog if it does not come right away.

Ⓑ Never scold your dog or punish your dog if it does not come right away.

Ⓒ Never scold or punish your dog if it does not come right away.

Ⓓ Scold or punish your dog if it never comes right away.

28. Which sentence would best fit at the end of this paragraph?

Ⓐ Some dogs can be very stubborn.

Ⓑ When the dog lies down, keep holding the leash.

Ⓒ You will quickly run out of treats if you're not careful.

Ⓓ Keep practicing until your dog learns to come when you call.

29. This paragraph was probably written for what audience?

Ⓐ dog owners

Ⓑ pet shop owners

Ⓒ animal doctors

Ⓓ dog catchers

Pretest

LANGUAGE ARTS: Study Skills

Directions: Choose the best answer to each question about finding information.

30. If you wanted to find an article about something that happened last week in France, you should look in –

   Ⓐ a world atlas

   Ⓑ a news magazine

   Ⓒ a French dictionary

   Ⓓ an encyclopedia

31. Which name would be listed first in alphabetical order?

   Ⓐ Toronto   Ⓒ Topeka

   Ⓑ Toledo   Ⓓ Tokyo

32. Which of these could be guide words on a dictionary page that includes the word *peacock?*

   Ⓐ patent/paw   Ⓒ pass/patch

   Ⓑ pawn/pearl   Ⓓ peak/pedal

33. To find out which of Scott O'Dell's books the library has, you should look in the –

   Ⓐ card catalog

   Ⓑ reference section

   Ⓒ telephone directory

   Ⓓ encyclopedia

Use the diagram to answer question 34.

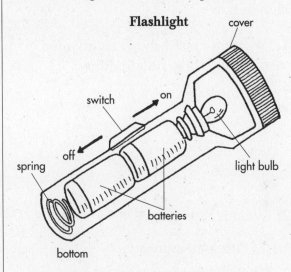

34. The bottom battery rests on the –

   Ⓐ light bulb   Ⓒ cover

   Ⓑ switch   Ⓓ spring

35. To find the meaning of a difficult word in a textbook, you should look in the –

   Ⓐ table of contents

   Ⓑ introduction

   Ⓒ glossary

   Ⓓ index

36. Which key word should you use when looking in an enclyclopedia for information about cobras, which are poisonous snakes in Africa?

   Ⓐ cobra   Ⓒ snakes

   Ⓑ poisonous   Ⓓ Africa

Stop

Pretest

MATHEMATICS: Concepts and Applications

Directions: Choose the best answer to each question.

1. Which numeral shows eighty-nine thousand three hundred fifty?

   (A) 890,350

   (B) 89,350

   (C) 89,305

   (D) 8935

2. What is the value of the **4** in 64,358?

   (A) 4 ten thousands

   (B) 4 thousands

   (C) 4 hundreds

   (D) 4 tens

3. Which numeral has the least value?

   (A) 1572   (C) 1725

   (B) 1752   (D) 1527

4. What is 6779 rounded to the nearest hundred?

   (A) 6800   (C) 6770

   (B) 6780   (D) 6700

5. Which number comes next in this pattern?

   7, 13, 20, 28, __?__ . . .

   (A) 37   (C) 39

   (B) 38   (D) 40

6. Which is an odd number?

   (A) 124   (C) 148

   (B) 137   (D) 166

7. Which is a factor of 27?

   (A) 6   (C) 8

   (B) 7   (D) 9

8. Which is the greatest common factor of 24 and 30?

   (A) 2   (C) 6

   (B) 3   (D) 8

9. Which is a multiple of 7?

   (A) 47   (C) 72

   (B) 63   (D) 81

10. What fractional part is shaded?

   (A) $\frac{1}{4}$ (C) $\frac{1}{2}$

   (B) $\frac{1}{3}$ (D) $\frac{3}{4}$

Go On

11. Which fraction is equivalent to $\frac{5}{15}$?

Ⓐ $\frac{1}{5}$ Ⓒ $\frac{3}{5}$

Ⓑ $\frac{1}{3}$ Ⓓ $\frac{2}{3}$

12. Which fraction is greatest?

Ⓐ $\frac{2}{4}$ Ⓒ $\frac{4}{5}$

Ⓑ $\frac{8}{12}$ Ⓓ $\frac{5}{7}$

13. Which decimal number is equivalent to $\frac{5}{100}$?

Ⓐ 50.0   Ⓒ 0.5

Ⓑ 5.0   Ⓓ 0.05

14. Which decimal number has the greateast value?

Ⓐ 30.0   Ⓒ 3.0

Ⓑ 0.03   Ⓓ 0.30

15. Which number is the arrow pointing to on the number line?

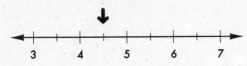

Ⓐ 4.0   Ⓒ 4.5

Ⓑ 4.1   Ⓓ 5.0

16. Which number completes both number sentences?

$12 \div 6 = \square$ $\square \times 5 = 10$

Ⓐ 2   Ⓒ 5

Ⓑ 3   Ⓓ 6

17. Choose the missing sign.

$120 \ \square \ 12 = 10$

$+$ $-$ $\times$ $\div$

Ⓐ   Ⓑ   Ⓒ   Ⓓ

18. Which point on the grid represents $(3, 2)$?

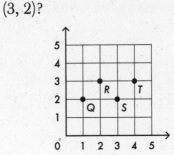

Q   R   S   T

Ⓐ   Ⓑ   Ⓒ   Ⓓ

19. Which figure below is a pyramid?

Ⓐ   Ⓒ

Ⓑ   Ⓓ

20. What is the diameter of a circle with a radius of 2 cm?

Ⓐ 1 cm   Ⓒ 4 cm

Ⓑ 2 cm   Ⓓ 8 cm

13

21. Which line is perpendicular to $\overleftrightarrow{AB}$?

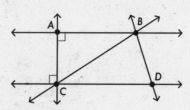

Ⓐ $\overleftrightarrow{BC}$

Ⓑ $\overleftrightarrow{BD}$

Ⓒ $\overleftrightarrow{AC}$

Ⓓ $\overleftrightarrow{CD}$

22. Which figure shows a line of symmetry?

 Ⓐ

 Ⓒ

 Ⓑ

 Ⓓ

23. What is the volume of this box?

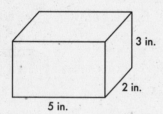

Ⓐ 6 in.^{3} Ⓒ 20 in.^{3}

Ⓑ 10 in.^{3} Ⓓ 30 in.^{3}

24. What is the perimeter of this rectangular field?

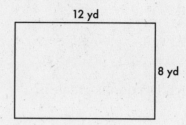

Ⓐ 20 yd   Ⓒ 40 yd

Ⓑ 28 yd   Ⓓ 96 yd

25. Which figure shows a right angle?

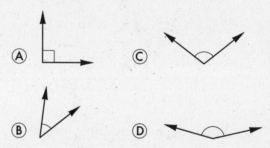

26. What is the area of this rectangular parking space?

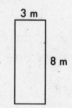

Ⓐ 11 m^2

Ⓑ 22 m^2

Ⓒ 24 m^2

Ⓓ 48 m^2

Go On

Directions: Solve each problem. If the correct answer is Not Given, mark answer D, "NG."

27. On Sunday Joel played tennis from 10:30 A.M. until 2:15 P.M. How long did he play?

Ⓐ 2 hours 15 minutes

Ⓑ 3 hours 45 minutes

Ⓒ 4 hours 30 minutes

Ⓓ NG

28. Five friends paid equal shares to buy a pizza for $14.95. Which number sentence should you use to find how much each friend paid?

Ⓐ $5.00 + $14.95 = □

Ⓑ $14.95 ÷ 5 = □

Ⓒ 5 × $14.95 = □

Ⓓ $14.95 − $5.00 = □

29. Kay bought three notebooks for $2.89 each. How much change should she get from a ten-dollar bill?

Ⓐ $1.33

Ⓑ $4.22

Ⓒ $8.67

Ⓓ NG

30. Trevor went to a baseball game that started at 2:10. What else do you need to know to find what time the game ended?

Ⓐ what teams were playing

Ⓑ who won the game

Ⓒ how long the game lasted

Ⓓ where the game was played

31. Casey put 178 marbles in 3 jars as equally as possible. <u>About</u> how many marbles did she put in each jar?

Ⓐ 50   Ⓒ 70

Ⓑ 60   Ⓓ 80

32. Peter has these test scores: 97, 85, 93, 77. What is the average of all his scores?

Ⓐ 80   Ⓒ 88

Ⓑ 85   Ⓓ NG

This graph shows how much time Suzy spent on homework in each subject in 1 week. Use the graph to answer questions 33–34.

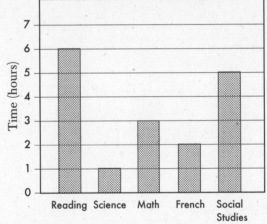

Time Spent on Homework

33. Which subject took exactly twice as long as Math?

Ⓐ Reading   Ⓒ French

Ⓑ Science   Ⓓ Social Studies

34. How much more time did Suzy spend on Social Studies than on Science and French together?

Ⓐ 7 hours   Ⓒ 3 hours

Ⓑ 5 hours   Ⓓ 2 hours

Stop

Pretest

MATHEMATICS: Computation

Directions: Find the answer to each problem. If the answer is Not Given, choose answer D, "NG."

35. $\frac{3}{4} - \frac{2}{3} =$

Ⓐ $\frac{6}{12}$

Ⓑ $\frac{1}{12}$

Ⓒ $\frac{1}{3}$

Ⓓ NG

36. $176.39
− 23.52

Ⓐ $152.87

Ⓑ $152.97

Ⓒ $153.87

Ⓓ NG

37. 251
× 6

Ⓐ 1206

Ⓑ 1236

Ⓒ 1606

Ⓓ NG

38. $562.74
+ 243.17

Ⓐ $805.91

Ⓑ $795.91

Ⓒ $795.81

Ⓓ NG

39. $\frac{1}{5}$
$+ \frac{1}{2}$

Ⓐ $\frac{7}{10}$

Ⓑ $\frac{3}{10}$

Ⓒ $\frac{1}{7}$

Ⓓ NG

40. $7\overline{)497}$

Ⓐ 701

Ⓑ 77

Ⓒ 71

Ⓓ NG

41. $203 + 359 =$

Ⓐ 462

Ⓑ 552

Ⓒ 562

Ⓓ NG

42. $13 \times 27 =$

Ⓐ 351

Ⓑ 331

Ⓒ 281

Ⓓ NG

43. $347 \div 23 =$

Ⓐ 15

Ⓑ 15 R2

Ⓒ 15 R5

Ⓓ NG

44. 3284
− 185

Ⓐ 1434

Ⓑ 3109

Ⓒ 3199

Ⓓ NG

45. $7.79 \times 5 =$

Ⓐ $389.50

Ⓑ $38.95

Ⓒ $3.89

Ⓓ NG

16

Stop

Reading

PRACTICE 1 • Synonyms and Antonyms

SAMPLES

Directions: Choose the word or words that mean the same, or almost the same, as the underlined word.

    A. People sometimes <u>abandon</u> their pets. <u>Abandon</u> means –

        Ⓐ train

        Ⓑ leave

        Ⓒ welcome

        Ⓓ feed

Directions: Choose the word that means the OPPOSITE of the underlined word.

    B. a <u>dangerous</u> trip

        Ⓐ safe

        Ⓑ risky

        Ⓒ long

        Ⓓ exciting

Tips and Reminders

- Words with the same meaning are *synonyms*. Watch out for answer choices that fit the sentence (such as *train* and *feed*) but have different meanings.

- Words with opposite meanings are *antonyms*. When looking for an antonym, watch out for words that have the same meaning (such as *risky*).

PRACTICE

Directions: Choose the word or words that mean the same, or almost the same, as the underlined word.

1. There was a <u>crater</u> in Gina's tooth. A <u>crater</u> is a –

    Ⓐ cookie

    Ⓑ hole

    Ⓒ filling

    Ⓓ pain

2. The mouse ate a <u>morsel</u> of cheese. A <u>morsel</u> is a –

    Ⓐ package

    Ⓑ small piece

    Ⓒ slice

    Ⓓ large chunk

Go On →

3. The robber <u>disguised</u> his real plan.
   <u>Disguised</u> means –

   Ⓐ hid
   Ⓑ found
   Ⓒ stole
   Ⓓ returned

4. The changes were <u>apparent</u>.
   <u>Apparent</u> means –

   Ⓐ serious
   Ⓑ difficult
   Ⓒ incorrect
   Ⓓ clear

5. Who came up with that <u>scheme</u>?
   A <u>scheme</u> is a –

   Ⓐ joke
   Ⓑ plan
   Ⓒ menu
   Ⓓ timetable

6. The knights held a <u>tournament</u>.
   A <u>tournament</u> is a –

   Ⓐ contest
   Ⓑ battle
   Ⓒ banner
   Ⓓ feast

7. Try to <u>concentrate</u> on your work.
   <u>Concentrate</u> means –

   Ⓐ focus
   Ⓑ improve
   Ⓒ score
   Ⓓ save

8. He expressed his <u>gratitude</u>.
   <u>Gratitude</u> is –

   Ⓐ sympathy
   Ⓑ happiness
   Ⓒ sorrow
   Ⓓ thanks

9. The <u>annual</u> picnic is this weekend.
   <u>Annual</u> means –

   Ⓐ nightly
   Ⓑ outdoor
   Ⓒ fall
   Ⓓ yearly

10. She did not find any <u>evidence</u>.
    <u>Evidence</u> means –

    Ⓐ entrance
    Ⓑ signs
    Ⓒ path
    Ⓓ view

11. Jim made a loud <u>declaration</u>.
    A <u>declaration</u> is a –

    Ⓐ noise
    Ⓑ sneeze
    Ⓒ statement
    Ⓓ question

12. He suffered from <u>exhaustion</u>.
    <u>Exhaustion</u> is –

    Ⓐ great tiredness
    Ⓑ difficult exercise
    Ⓒ lack of movement
    Ⓓ great sadness

Go On

PRACTICE 1 • Synonyms and Antonyms (continued)

Directions: Choose the word that means the OPPOSITE of the underlined word.

13. valuable information
    - Ⓐ interesting
    - Ⓑ worthless
    - Ⓒ amusing
    - Ⓓ detailed

14. sensible clothing
    - Ⓐ expensive
    - Ⓑ warm
    - Ⓒ foolish
    - Ⓓ woolen

15. wither outdoors
    - Ⓐ thrive
    - Ⓑ freeze
    - Ⓒ sunburn
    - Ⓓ cook

16. depart soon
    - Ⓐ leave
    - Ⓑ exit
    - Ⓒ arrive
    - Ⓓ follow

17. criticize loudly
    - Ⓐ complain
    - Ⓑ praise
    - Ⓒ discuss
    - Ⓓ talk

18. describe accurately
    - Ⓐ exactly
    - Ⓑ slowly
    - Ⓒ unexpectedly
    - Ⓓ incorrectly

19. a disastrous trip
    - Ⓐ business
    - Ⓑ comfortable
    - Ⓒ camping
    - Ⓓ successful

20. innocent person
    - Ⓐ helpful
    - Ⓑ friendly
    - Ⓒ guilty
    - Ⓓ sorry

21. a prompt reply
    - Ⓐ slow
    - Ⓑ quick
    - Ⓒ swift
    - Ⓓ rude

22. a sturdy desk
    - Ⓐ solid
    - Ⓑ flimsy
    - Ⓒ steady
    - Ⓓ wooden

Stop

Language Arts

PRACTICE 2 • Using Verbs

Directions: Read each sentence and look at the underlined word or words. There may be a mistake in word usage. If you find a mistake, choose the best way to write the underlined part of the sentence. If there is no mistake, fill in the bubble beside answer D, "Correct as is."

SAMPLES

A. Two cars <u>is parked</u> on the side of the road.

    Ⓐ has parked
    Ⓑ are parked
    Ⓒ was parked
    Ⓓ Correct as is

B. Ms. Ames <u>teached</u> us to read a weather map.

    Ⓐ taught
    Ⓑ teachered
    Ⓒ has teached
    Ⓓ Correct as is

Tips and Reminders

- Try each answer choice in the sentence to see which one sounds right.

- Be careful with irregular forms of verbs, such as *taught*, *threw*, and *became*.

- Watch out for answer choices that are not real words, such as *teachered*.

PRACTICE

1. Every day Al <u>exercise</u> for 20 minutes.

    Ⓐ exercising
    Ⓑ exercises
    Ⓒ were exercising
    Ⓓ Correct as is

2. Apples <u>are ripening</u> late this year.

    Ⓐ were ripened
    Ⓑ are ripen
    Ⓒ was ripening
    Ⓓ Correct as is

Go On

3. A hummingbird <u>fluttering</u> its wings faster than the eye can see.

  (A) flutter

  (B) does flutters

  (C) flutters

  (D) Correct as is

4. One of my friends <u>call</u> me every day.

  (A) calls

  (B) were calling

  (C) have called

  (D) Correct as is

5. Joseph <u>has took</u> that path in the woods before.

  (A) taken

  (B) has taken

  (C) was taken

  (D) Correct as is

6. Carolyn <u>drink</u> her milk quickly and got hiccups.

  (A) drank

  (B) drinked

  (C) has drank

  (D) Correct as is

7. The water level <u>rised</u> to the second floor during the storm.

  (A) rose

  (B) risen

  (C) raised

  (D) Correct as is

8. I <u>have never swum</u> in a quarry.

  (A) have never swam

  (B) have never swimmed

  (C) has never swum

  (D) Correct as is

9. Jeff and his sister <u>was</u> late.

  (A) is

  (B) be

  (C) were

  (D) Correct as is

10. Buster <u>shaked</u> himself to dry his fur.

  (A) shooked

  (B) shook

  (C) shaken

  (D) Correct as is

11. Everybody <u>is coming</u> to the party tonight.

  (A) were coming

  (B) are coming

  (C) is come

  (D) Correct as is

12. The hurricane <u>blowed</u> all the leaves off the trees.

  (A) blowing

  (B) blow

  (C) blew

  (D) Correct as is

 Stop

Mathematics

PRACTICE 3 • Whole Number Concepts

Directions: Choose the best answer to each question.

SAMPLES

A. Which numeral shows sixty-one thousand two hundred thirty?

  Ⓐ 6123

  Ⓑ 6230

  Ⓒ 61,203

  Ⓓ 61,230

B. What is the value of the **6** in 12,650?

  Ⓐ 6 tens

  Ⓑ 6 hundreds

  Ⓒ 6 thousands

  Ⓓ 6 ten thousands

C. Which is a multiple of 12?

  Ⓐ 122

  Ⓑ 96

  Ⓒ 21

  Ⓓ 4

D. What is 8173 rounded to the nearest hundred?

  Ⓐ 8000

  Ⓑ 8100

  Ⓒ 8170

  Ⓓ 8200

Tips and Reminders

• Be sure to look at all the answer choices. Try each answer choice to find the one that is correct.

• After choosing an answer, read the question again to make sure you have answered it correctly.

PRACTICE

1. Which numeral shows fifty-two thousand three hundred seven?

  Ⓐ 50,237

  Ⓑ 52,370

  Ⓒ 52,307

  Ⓓ 52,037

2. What number is missing?

  36, 27, __?__, 9 . . .

  Ⓐ 21

  Ⓑ 19

  Ⓒ 18

  Ⓓ 12

Go On

3. Which of these is a factor of 56?

(A) 6

(B) 8

(C) 11

(D) 12

4. What is 57,842 rounded to the nearest ten thousand?

(A) 50,000

(B) 57,000

(C) 58,000

(D) 60,000

5. What is the greatest common factor of 132 and 96?

(A) 8

(B) 12

(C) 24

(D) 32

6. Which figure should come next in the pattern?

(A) ●   (C) ⬢

(B) ■   (D) ▲

7. What is the value of the 4 in 34,089?

(A) 4 tens

(B) 4 hundreds

(C) 4 thousands

(D) 4 ten thousands

8. Which is a multiple of 13?

(A) 29

(B) 49

(C) 51

(D) 78

9. Which is an even number?

(A) 723

(B) 409

(C) 530

(D) 621

10. Which number has the greatest value?

(A) 5310

(B) 5301

(C) 5031

(D) 5013

11. Which number has the least value?

(A) 102,659

(B) 120,569

(C) 102,965

(D) 201,569

12. Which address is an odd number?

(A) 4102 Main Street

(B) 4201 Main Street

(C) 4012 Main Street

(D) 4120 Main Street

Stop

Reading

PRACTICE 4 • Context Clues

SAMPLES

Directions: Read the sentences. Choose the word that best completes both sentences.

A. There is a dark _____ on the rug.

Did you _____ any unusual birds?

- (A) stain
- (B) color
- (C) catch
- (D) spot

Directions: Read the sentences. Choose the word that best fits in the blank.

I was __(B)__ to see a clown drive down the street. Then I remembered that the circus had come to town.

- **B.** (A) surprised
- (B) bothered
- (C) looking
- (D) anxious

Tips and Reminders

- Think of the different meanings you know for each word. Watch out for words that fit one sentence but not the other.

- Read the whole paragraph first. Try each answer choice in the sentence to see which one sounds right.

PRACTICE

Directions: Read the sentences. Choose the word that best completes both sentences.

1. Use a whisk to _____ the egg whites until they are fluffy.

Lou began to _____ the drum in time to the music.

- (A) stir
- (B) beat
- (C) pound
- (D) mix

2. You need to _____ the boxes flat for recycling.

Alice has a _____ on the boy next door.

- (A) mash
- (B) squeeze
- (C) level
- (D) crush

Go On

3. Please _____ the candle.

   Jennifer has _____ brown hair.

   Ⓐ snuff
   Ⓑ light
   Ⓒ dark
   Ⓓ long

4. Could you give me a _____ with the dishes?

   He wore a ring on his left _____.

   Ⓐ hand
   Ⓑ side
   Ⓒ finger
   Ⓓ toe

5. You _____ yourself well in writing.

   Joe took the _____ train to the city.

   Ⓐ describe
   Ⓑ explain
   Ⓒ express
   Ⓓ local

6. The president will _____ the meeting.

   Did you _____ the window?

   Ⓐ lead
   Ⓑ open
   Ⓒ set
   Ⓓ chair

7. This news will _____ you.

   I got a _____ when I touched the light.

   Ⓐ shock
   Ⓑ startle
   Ⓒ cheer
   Ⓓ charge

8. Just _____ the right button.

   I have to _____ my pants.

   Ⓐ push
   Ⓑ press
   Ⓒ iron
   Ⓓ crease

9. What did you _____ in the garden?

   My father works at the _____.

   Ⓐ grow
   Ⓑ factory
   Ⓒ shop
   Ⓓ plant

10. The figure skater began to _____.

    Miko wants to go for a _____ in her new car.

    Ⓐ turn
    Ⓑ ride
    Ⓒ spin
    Ⓓ twirl

Go On →

Directions: Read the paragraph. Choose the word that best fits in each blank.

Have you ever heard of a town holding a food fight? Every year in July, thousands of tourists __(11)__ to the town of Buñol, Spain, to participate in the *Tomatina*. Hundreds of tons of ripe tomatoes are trucked into Buñol from __(12)__ farm communities. When a signal is given, people __(13)__ the ripe vegetables at one another. What a __(14)__ the town must be after that event!

11. (A) flow
    (B) write
    (C) reserve
    (D) travel

13. (A) eat
    (B) grow
    (C) hurl
    (D) splatter

12. (A) surrounding
    (B) dairy
    (C) irrigated
    (D) faraway

14. (A) jam
    (B) mess
    (C) view
    (D) sauce

Scientists have recently __(15)__ a 5400-year-old mound in Louisiana. This is the oldest man-made structure in North America and is even older than some of the Egyptian pyramids. The 300-yard wide circular mound suggests that not all early Americans lived simply by hunting and gathering. Scientists __(16)__ that people with enough free time to build such large structures also had plenty of food in storage and a well-organized society.

15. (A) buried
    (B) discovered
    (C) built
    (D) invented

16. (A) predict
    (B) believe
    (C) direct
    (D) hope

Stop

Language Arts

PRACTICE 5 • Grammar and Usage

Directions: Read each sentence and look at the underlined word or words. There may be a mistake in word usage. If you find a mistake, choose the best way to write the underlined part of the sentence. If there is no mistake, fill in the bubble beside answer D, "Correct as is."

SAMPLES

A. <u>Jeff and me</u> are having a contest.

- (A) Me and Jeff
- (B) Jeff and us
- (C) Jeff and I
- (D) Correct as is

B. Of all the gifts I received, Theo's gift was the <u>more unusual</u>.

- (A) more unusualer
- (B) most unusual
- (C) unusualest
- (D) Correct as is

> **Tips and Reminders**
> - Try each answer choice in the sentence to see which one sounds right.
> - Watch out for answer choices that are not really words, such as *unusualer*.

PRACTICE

1. Shirley <u>hardly never</u> watches TV.

- (A) not hardly ever
- (B) hardly ever
- (C) not hardly never
- (D) Correct as is

2. I have a new ski hat somewhere, but I can't find <u>him</u>.

- (A) it
- (B) them
- (C) her
- (D) Correct as is

Go On →

3. Cats are <u>most curious</u> than dogs.

Ⓐ curiouser

Ⓑ most curiouser

Ⓒ more curious

Ⓓ Correct as is

4. The twins made a doghouse for <u>they</u> pet.

Ⓐ its

Ⓑ their

Ⓒ theirs

Ⓓ Correct as is

5. Mike is the <u>silliest</u> person I know.

Ⓐ sillier

Ⓑ most silly

Ⓒ most silliest

Ⓓ Correct as is

6. Could I have <u>a</u> apple?

Ⓐ an

Ⓑ those

Ⓒ these

Ⓓ Correct as is

7. Grandma <u>doesn't</u> like peanuts.

Ⓐ doesn't not

Ⓑ won't not

Ⓒ can't not

Ⓓ Correct as is

8. <u>That lion it</u> roared at us.

Ⓐ The lion it

Ⓑ It that lion

Ⓒ That lion

Ⓓ Correct as is

9. The temperature is supposed to be <u>more warmer</u> today than yesterday.

Ⓐ warmest

Ⓑ warmer

Ⓒ most warmer

Ⓓ Correct as is

10. November is cold enough, but December is <u>worser</u>.

Ⓐ worse

Ⓑ worst

Ⓒ more worse

Ⓓ Correct as is

11. Did you throw out <u>the</u> newspaper?

Ⓐ an

Ⓑ these

Ⓒ its

Ⓓ Correct as is

12. We gave the award to <u>she</u>.

Ⓐ he

Ⓑ her

Ⓒ they

Ⓓ Correct as is

Stop

Mathematics

PRACTICE 6 • Fractions and Decimals

Directions: Choose the best answer to each question.

SAMPLES

A. Which decimal number is greatest?

- Ⓐ 171.7
- Ⓑ 0.1717
- Ⓒ 17.17
- Ⓓ 1.717

B. Which fraction is equivalent to $\frac{6}{10}$?

- Ⓐ $\frac{1}{6}$
- Ⓒ $\frac{3}{10}$
- Ⓑ $\frac{3}{6}$
- Ⓓ $\frac{3}{5}$

> **Tips and Reminders**
>
> - To compare fractions, change them to "like" fractions with the same denominator.
> - To compare decimal numbers, line up the decimal points.

PRACTICE

1. Which fraction is another name for $\frac{8}{12}$?

- Ⓐ $\frac{1}{2}$
- Ⓒ $\frac{3}{4}$
- Ⓑ $\frac{2}{3}$
- Ⓓ $\frac{4}{8}$

2. What number does the arrow point to on the number line?

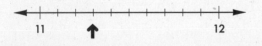

- Ⓐ 11.2
- Ⓑ 11.3
- Ⓒ 11.5
- Ⓓ 11.6

3. Marvin used $\frac{2}{3}$ gallon of white paint, $\frac{5}{6}$ gallon of blue, $\frac{1}{2}$ gallon of red, and $\frac{7}{8}$ gallon of yellow. Which color did he use the most?

- Ⓐ white
- Ⓒ blue
- Ⓑ red
- Ⓓ yellow

4. Which set of decimal numbers is ordered from least to greatest?

- Ⓐ 2.67, 267.0, 26.7, 0.267
- Ⓑ 2.67, 26.7, 0.267, 267.0
- Ⓒ 0.267, 2.67, 26.7, 267.0
- Ⓓ 267.0, 26.7, 2.67, 0.267

Go On

5. Which decimal number is equal to $\frac{4}{5}$?

Ⓐ 0.8

Ⓑ 0.6

Ⓒ 0.5

Ⓓ 0.4

6. $0.25 is what fraction of one dollar?

Ⓐ $\frac{1}{5}$

Ⓑ $\frac{1}{4}$

Ⓒ $\frac{1}{3}$

Ⓓ $\frac{1}{2}$

7. Which fractional part is shaded?

Ⓐ $\frac{1}{3}$

Ⓑ $\frac{1}{4}$

Ⓒ $\frac{1}{2}$

Ⓓ $\frac{1}{12}$

8. Which fraction is equivalent to $\frac{4}{16}$?

Ⓐ $\frac{1}{2}$

Ⓑ $\frac{1}{4}$

Ⓒ $\frac{2}{12}$

Ⓓ $\frac{3}{8}$

9. Clarice and her friends had 4 pizzas. They ate $\frac{5}{8}$ of the pepperoni pizza, $\frac{3}{8}$ of the mushroom, $\frac{1}{2}$ of the cheese, and $\frac{3}{4}$ of the sausage. Of which pizza did they eat the least?

Ⓐ pepperoni

Ⓑ cheese

Ⓒ sausage

Ⓓ mushroom

10. The arrow points to what number on the number line?

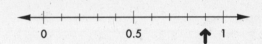

Ⓐ 0.6

Ⓑ 0.8

Ⓒ 0.9

Ⓓ 1.1

11. What fraction of one dollar is $0.90?

Ⓐ $\frac{1}{9}$

Ⓑ $\frac{1}{10}$

Ⓒ $\frac{5}{9}$

Ⓓ $\frac{9}{10}$

12. Which amount is greatest?

Ⓐ $1.10

Ⓑ $0.11

Ⓒ $1.01

Ⓓ $0.10

Stop

Reading

PRACTICE 7 • Word Analysis

SAMPLES

Directions: Choose the word or phrase that gives the meaning of the underlined prefix or suffix.

A. <u>semi</u>circle   <u>semi</u>annual

   (A) twice

   (B) half

   (C) above

   (D) toward

B. fear<u>less</u>   worth<u>less</u>

   (A) filled with

   (B) after

   (C) without

   (D) before

Directions: Read the sentence and the question. Choose the word that best answers the question.

C. Alex was _____ to find a job. Which word suggests that he would not give up easily?

   (A) expecting   (C) excited

   (B) hoping   (D) determined

Directions: Read the meaning of the original word. Then choose the modern word that comes from the original word.

D. Which word probably comes from the Middle English word *dreynen*, meaning "to filter"?

   (A) drain   (C) drawer

   (B) drying   (D) dreamer

Tips and Reminders

- A prefix is a word part added to the beginning of a word, as in *unkind* and *repaint*.

- A suffix is a word part added to the end of a word, as in *nearly* and *careful*.

- The *connotation* of a word is the meaning that it suggests. To find the correct connotation, think about the suggested meaning of each word.

- To find the modern word that comes from the original word, look carefully at the spelling of each answer choice and think about what it means.

PRACTICE

Directions: Choose the word or phrase that gives the meaning of the underlined prefix or suffix.

1. <u>in</u>active   <u>in</u>correct

   Ⓐ partly
   Ⓑ not
   Ⓒ again
   Ⓓ very

2. <u>pre</u>plan   <u>pre</u>view

   Ⓐ against
   Ⓑ inside
   Ⓒ before
   Ⓓ on

3. amuse<u>ment</u>   amaze<u>ment</u>

   Ⓐ opposed to
   Ⓑ state or quality of
   Ⓒ without
   Ⓓ one who

4. gold<u>en</u>   wood<u>en</u>

   Ⓐ nearly
   Ⓑ not
   Ⓒ made of
   Ⓓ the study of

Directions: Read the sentence and the question. Choose the word that best answers the question.

5. The crowd _____ as the singer finished performing.
   Which word suggests that the crowd did not like the singing?

   Ⓐ jeered   Ⓒ applauded
   Ⓑ cheered   Ⓓ yawned

6. The bear _____ toward the beehive. Which word suggests that the bear moved awkwardly?

   Ⓐ lumbered   Ⓒ trotted
   Ⓑ scampered   Ⓓ skipped

Directions: Read the meaning of the original word. Then choose the modern word that comes from the original word.

7. Which word probably comes from the Old French word *coucoun*, meaning "eggshell"?

   Ⓐ cocoa   Ⓒ cocoon
   Ⓑ count   Ⓓ course

8. Which word probably comes from the Middle English word *net*, meaning "clean"?

   Ⓐ neat   Ⓒ network
   Ⓑ neither   Ⓓ neighbor

Stop

Language Arts

PRACTICE 8 • Sentences

SAMPLES

Directions: Choose the simple subject of the sentence.

A. <u>Omar's</u> <u>brother</u> <u>went</u> to a yard <u>sale</u>.
   Ⓐ   Ⓑ   Ⓒ   Ⓓ

Directions: Choose the simple predicate of the sentence.

B. <u>Becky</u> <u>often</u> <u>buys</u> used <u>furniture</u>.
   Ⓐ   Ⓑ   Ⓒ   Ⓓ

Directions: Find the answer that is a complete sentence written correctly.

C. Ⓐ Angela's name means "angel."

    Ⓑ Making you wonder if she should have a different name.

    Ⓒ Her brother's name is Jolly now that's a name that fits.

    Ⓓ Their parents named John and Mary.

Tips and Reminders

- To find the subject of a sentence, ask yourself *who* or *what* is doing something ("Omar's <u>brother</u> went . . .").

- To find the predicate of a sentence, ask yourself *what* the person or thing is doing ("Becky often <u>buys</u> . . .").

- A complete sentence has a subject and a verb and expresses a complete thought. Watch out for answers that include two sentences run together.

PRACTICE

Directions: Choose the simple subject of the sentence.

1. <u>This</u> new <u>cookbook</u> has a <u>recipe</u> for sauerkraut <u>cake</u>.
   Ⓐ   Ⓑ   Ⓒ   Ⓓ

2. A blue <u>moon</u> <u>occurs</u> <u>once</u> in a great <u>while</u>.
       Ⓐ   Ⓑ   Ⓒ   Ⓓ

3. Our <u>school's</u> jump <u>rope</u> <u>team</u> won a national <u>contest</u>.
    Ⓐ   Ⓑ   Ⓒ   Ⓓ

Go On →

Directions: Choose the simple predicate of the sentence.

4. <u>She</u> <u>learned</u> how to <u>lasso</u> at a dude <u>ranch</u>.
   Ⓐ   Ⓑ   Ⓒ   Ⓓ

5. Before <u>getting</u> a <u>license</u>, <u>Maggie</u> <u>took</u> a driving test.
         Ⓐ   Ⓑ   Ⓒ   Ⓓ

6. There <u>are</u> several <u>mountains</u> in New Hampshire <u>named</u> after <u>presidents</u>.
       Ⓐ   Ⓑ   Ⓒ   Ⓓ

Directions: Find the answer that is a complete sentence written correctly.

7. Ⓐ Before painting, sanding all the rough spots.
   Ⓑ Putting quite a bit of paint on the brush.
   Ⓒ You should apply the paint with long even strokes.
   Ⓓ Wipe the end of the brush that way the paint won't drip.

8. Ⓐ Knowing what to do if your pet gets sprayed by a skunk.
   Ⓑ Tomato juice a common cure.
   Ⓒ Just use it as shampoo it takes away the smell.
   Ⓓ Be sure to wash out the tub!

9. Ⓐ Spaghetti squash being a very strange plant.
   Ⓑ A large yellow squash.
   Ⓒ After it's cooked, the inside looks like spaghetti.
   Ⓓ Put butter on it some people even use tomato sauce.

10. Ⓐ Some towns have a swap shop at the dump.
    Ⓑ Furniture, books, and records you don't want anymore.
    Ⓒ Somebody else with the perfect spot for your old lamp.
    Ⓓ Better than throwing everything into the landfill.

11. Ⓐ A costume for a costume party?
    Ⓑ You can start with a big empty carton.
    Ⓒ Paint it red and blue it becomes a mailbox.
    Ⓓ Wrapped with paper and a bow as a present.

12. Ⓐ There are many bits of folklore about nature.
    Ⓑ Seeing a ring around the moon.
    Ⓒ Moss on the north side of trees.
    Ⓓ Cows lie down before it rains they face away from the wind.

Stop

Mathematics

PRACTICE 9 • Number Operations

Directions: Choose the best answer to each question.

SAMPLES

A. Which number goes in the box to complete the number sentence?

$25 \times \square = 10 \times 10$

Ⓐ 3

Ⓑ 4

Ⓒ 5

Ⓓ 20

B. Which sign goes in the circle?

$9 + 9 = 36 \bigcirc 2$

$+$ $-$ $\times$ $\div$

Ⓐ   Ⓑ   Ⓒ   Ⓓ

C. Which point on the grid represents (5, 3)?

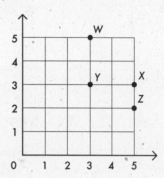

Ⓐ W   Ⓒ Y

Ⓑ X   Ⓓ Z

Tips and Reminders

• Read each number sentence carefully. Try each answer choice in the number sentence until you find one that is correct.

• In an ordered pair, find the first number by counting to the right. The second number tells how many spaces to count up.

PRACTICE

1. Which number makes this number sentence true?

$15 \times \square = 2 \times 75$

5   10   25   50

Ⓐ   Ⓑ   Ⓒ   Ⓓ

2. What is another way to write 3×7?

Ⓐ $3 + 7$

Ⓑ $7 \times 7 \times 7$

Ⓒ $(3 \times 3) + (7 \times 7)$

Ⓓ $7 + 7 + 7$

Go On

3. Which sign goes in the circle?

$27 \bigcirc 3 = 12 - 3$

$+$ $\quad$ $-$ $\quad$ $\times$ $\quad$ $\div$
Ⓐ $\quad$ Ⓑ $\quad$ Ⓒ $\quad$ Ⓓ

4. What coordinates are shown by the point on the grid?

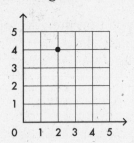

Ⓐ (2, 4) $\qquad$ Ⓒ (3, 5)
Ⓑ (4, 2) $\qquad$ Ⓓ (5, 3)

5. Which number makes this number sentence true?

$49 - 4 = \square \times 5$

6 $\quad$ 7 $\quad$ 8 $\quad$ 9
Ⓐ $\quad$ Ⓑ $\quad$ Ⓒ $\quad$ Ⓓ

6. If $n = 12$, then $n + 4 =$

Ⓐ 8
Ⓑ 16
Ⓒ 20
Ⓓ 48

7. Which sign goes in the circle?

$6 \bigcirc 19 = 30 - 5$

$+$ $\quad$ $-$ $\quad$ $\times$ $\quad$ $\div$
Ⓐ $\quad$ Ⓑ $\quad$ Ⓒ $\quad$ Ⓓ

8. If $56 + x = 70$, then $x =$

Ⓐ 14
Ⓑ 16
Ⓒ 24
Ⓓ 126

9. Which sign goes in the circle?

$100 \bigcirc 1 = 5 \times 20$

$+$ $\quad$ $-$ $\quad$ $\times$ $\quad$ $\div$
Ⓐ $\quad$ Ⓑ $\quad$ Ⓒ $\quad$ Ⓓ

10. What number goes in the box to make the number sentence true?

$135 + (28 + 49) = (135 + 28) + \square$

163 $\quad$ 77 $\quad$ 49 $\quad$ 28
Ⓐ $\quad$ Ⓑ $\quad$ Ⓒ $\quad$ Ⓓ

11. Which point on the grid represents (0, 4)?

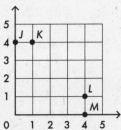

J $\quad$ K $\quad$ L $\quad$ M
Ⓐ $\quad$ Ⓑ $\quad$ Ⓒ $\quad$ Ⓓ

12. Which number sentence is in the same family of facts as $35 \div 7 = 5$?

Ⓐ $35 - 7 = 28$
Ⓑ $5 \times 7 = 35$
Ⓒ $35 - 5 = 30$
Ⓓ $7 + 5 = 12$

Reading

PRACTICE 10 • Interpreting Text

SAMPLES

Directions: Read the passage. Then answer the questions that follow.

   Dinah and Rachel were trying to decide how to spend their money at the Chester Fair. Dinah mostly wanted to go on rides: the Twister, the Whip, and the Comet. Rachel said that rides made her stomach turn upside down. She wanted to win a stuffed frog by throwing a ball at a target.

   "Oh, Rachel," groaned Dinah. "Those games are such a fraud. They make it look easy to hit the target, but actually they're almost impossible. Besides, you don't need another stuffed animal. Your room is like a toy store already."

   "I know," said Rachel. "Let's get our faces painted instead."

   "Perfect," said Dinah with a face as bright as the lights on the Ferris wheel.

A. What did Rachel mean when she said her stomach would "turn upside down"?

   Ⓐ She would fall off the ride.

   Ⓑ She would get very hungry.

   Ⓒ She would feel very confused.

   Ⓓ She would feel sick.

B. In the second paragraph, the word <u>fraud</u> means –

   Ⓐ exciting time

   Ⓑ unfair trick

   Ⓒ expensive activity

   Ⓓ boring activity

Tips and Reminders

- For words you don't know, look in the passage for clues that can help you guess their meaning.

- If a sentence doesn't seem to make sense the way it is written, look for a "hidden" or implied meaning. Use context clues to help figure out what the sentence really means.

Go On →

PRACTICE

Matthew loved reading about world records. He had memorized the height of the tallest man in the world and the weight of the fattest hamster. He could tell you the duration of the world's longest game of musical chairs and the greatest number of marshmallows ever eaten at a single sitting. He knew the identity of the world's oldest driver, and he could tell you where the world's longest scarf had been knitted.

Names, places, and numbers buzzed inside Matthew's brain like a swarm of mosquitoes. Once when his teacher asked him the answer to 72 divided by 9, Matthew rejoined, "8192." It turned out he was thinking about the world record number of noodles made in one minute.

"Matthew," said his teacher, "if you don't stop dreaming and put your nose to the grindstone, you are going to set the record for wrong answers in this class."

1. In the first paragraph, the word <u>duration</u> means –

   Ⓐ location
   Ⓑ length
   Ⓒ winner
   Ⓓ date

2. "Names, places, and numbers buzzed inside Matthew's brain like a swarm of mosquitoes" means that Matthew –

   Ⓐ had gotten sick from a mosquito bite
   Ⓑ could never remember anything
   Ⓒ had a mind full of odd facts
   Ⓓ had a hearing problem

3. In the second paragraph, the word <u>rejoined</u> means –

   Ⓐ answered
   Ⓑ connected
   Ⓒ forgot
   Ⓓ agreed

4. Matthew must "put his nose to the grindstone" means that he must –

   Ⓐ work harder
   Ⓑ accept his punishment
   Ⓒ leave the class
   Ⓓ relax and stop worrying

Go On

It was 7:30 A.M. In just eight minutes, the school bus would pull up to the bus stop opposite Neal's house. Neal searched frantically through the debris under his bed. Was that his shoe lurking in the darkness? No, it was a sock, bunched up and covered with dustballs like a furry, gray caterpillar.

Neal checked the closet again. He had already looked under each of the shirts and pairs of jeans that lay on the floor, but he decided to check again. No luck. His watch said 7:33.

If only Mrs. Nash would be late, like last year's driver. Unfortunately, she was as reliable as a watch that never needed winding.

Neal dashed from one room to another. He was spinning like a top out of control. Where was that stupid shoe? If he didn't find it in the next three minutes, he'd have to hobble out to the bus in his snow boots. Since it was a warm day in September, he could just imagine the jokes.

5. In the first paragraph, the word <u>debris</u> means –

   Ⓐ caterpillar
   Ⓑ drawers
   Ⓒ shoes
   Ⓓ junk

6. Mrs. Nash was "as reliable as a watch that never needed winding" means that she –

   Ⓐ was always exactly on time
   Ⓑ often had to wind her watch
   Ⓒ had to watch the winding road
   Ⓓ was not very dependable

7. Neal was "spinning like a top out of control" means that he was –

   Ⓐ playing instead of looking for his shoe
   Ⓑ moving quickly and without direction
   Ⓒ in control of what he was doing
   Ⓓ looking on the top shelf for his shoes

8. The word <u>hobble</u> in the last paragraph refers to a way of –

   Ⓐ walking
   Ⓑ searching
   Ⓒ teasing
   Ⓓ yelling

Stop

Language Arts

PRACTICE 11 • Punctuation

Directions: Read the sentences. Choose the sentence that shows the correct punctuation.

SAMPLES

A. (A) Spiders use silk to make webs and capture their prey.

(B) What exactly is a wolf spider!

(C) Some spiders live underwater and eat tiny underwater creatures?

(D) What a scary sight a tarantula is?

B. (A) Our teacher asked us what we want to be when we grow up?

(B) Anns dream is to become a comedian.

(C) Jody said, I have no idea.

(D) Zack answered, "I want to be a reporter."

> **Tips and Reminders**
> - Check every punctuation mark. Decide if the mark is needed, and make sure it is the correct kind of punctuation.
> - Read each sentence to yourself to decide if it sounds right. If there is a pause in the sentence, there should be a punctuation mark.

PRACTICE

1. (A) Isabels mother works for a toy company.

(B) The company sells toys dolls, and children's books.

(C) Her mother's name is P T Barnes.

(D) She travels all over the world, and she loves her job.

2. (A) What invention changed the world the most?

(B) Some say that it was the television but I dont believe it.

(C) Others claim "it was the automobile."

(D) Perhaps, it was the printing press!

Go On

3. (A) Jonah said, "Let's join the swim team.

   (B) Hannah said, If we all practice on Wednesday, our moms can carpool.

   (C) Kelly moaned, "I have too many activities already."

   (D) Sarah said, "You aren't busy on Wednesdays, though.

4. (A) On January 24 1848, James Marshall found gold in California.

   (B) Soon Americans Europeans and Chinese, were rushing to California.

   (C) Some of the miners found gold, but few struck it rich.

   (D) Many people stayed in California and, soon it became a state.

5. (A) Every morning, the principal makes public announcements.

   (B) Today she said, "Shawn James please come to the office."

   (C) I couldnt think of anything I had done wrong!

   (D) It turns out I had won a prize for a silly poem called School Lunch.

6. (A) Yetta saw a vole a small rodent run into the garden.

   (B) She yelled, ran toward the garden, and scared it away.

   (C) Voles, and other animals, will eat the vegetables.

   (D) Yetta grows lettuce beets and carrots.

7. (A) Sharon moved here from Ames, Iowa.

   (B) She asked me, if there are any good after-school activities.

   (C) I recommended, field hockey the chess club and in-line skating.

   (D) I said that Ms. Park the gym teacher, is really nice.

8. (A) Everyone should know some first aid?

   (B) Have you ever taken a course!

   (C) My dad is a volunteer with the local fire department

   (D) How proud I am of him for helping so many people!

9. (A) "Jim what is your mothers name?" asked Sheila.

   (B) Jim replied, "My mother's name is J.L. Marks."

   (C) What do the initials stand for," Sheila asked.

   (D) "They stand for Jennifer Louise, said Jim."

10. (A) Yes, I've read the new library rules.

    (B) One rule says, that you can only take out four books at a time.

    (C) Mr. Carvey, the librarian made up the rules himself.

    (D) I dont think theyre fair at all.

Stop

Mathematics

PRACTICE 12 • Geometry

Directions: Choose the best answer to each question.

SAMPLES

A. How many angles does this figure have?

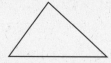

   (A) 3   (C) 5

   (B) 4   (D) 6

B. What is the area of this rectangle?

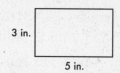

   (A) 8 in.^{2} (C) 16 in.^{2}

   (B) 15 in.^{2} (D) 30 in.^{2}

Tips and Reminders

- Use the pictures to find the information you need.
- After choosing an answer, read the question again to make sure you have answered it correctly.

PRACTICE

1. What part of the circle is labeled *a?*

   (A) radius

   (B) circumference

   (C) diameter

   (D) perimeter

2. Which is an acute angle?

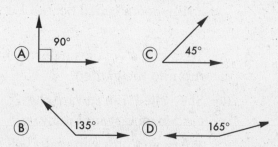

Go On

3. What is the name for the part of the circle shown by the dotted line?

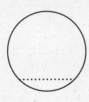

Ⓐ radius

Ⓑ diameter

Ⓒ chord

Ⓓ perimeter

4. Which figure is a rectangular pyramid?

Ⓐ   Ⓒ

Ⓑ   Ⓓ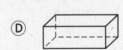

5. How many faces does this figure have?

Ⓐ 12   Ⓒ 6

Ⓑ 8   Ⓓ 4

6. Which figures are congruent?

Ⓐ figures F and G

Ⓑ figures G and H

Ⓒ figures G and J

Ⓓ figures F and H

7. Which figure shows a line of symmetry?

Ⓐ   Ⓒ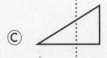

Ⓑ    Ⓓ

8. In which pair are the lines probably parallel?

Ⓐ 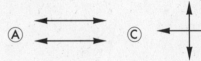   Ⓒ

Ⓑ    Ⓓ

9. If the radius of a circle is 8 cm, what is the diameter?

Ⓐ 2 cm   Ⓒ 6 cm

Ⓑ 4 cm   Ⓓ 16 cm

10. What is the perimeter of this rectangle?

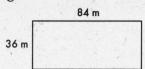

84 m

36 m

Ⓐ 36 m   Ⓒ 240 m

Ⓑ 84 m   Ⓓ 3224 m

11. What is the area of a square that measures 3 yd on one side?

Ⓐ 6 yd^2 Ⓒ 12 yd^2

Ⓑ 9 yd^2 Ⓓ 18 yd^2

12. How many vertices does this figure have?

Ⓐ 3   Ⓒ 5

Ⓑ 4   Ⓓ 6

13. What is the volume of this figure?

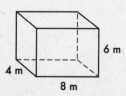

6 m

4 m

8 m

Ⓐ 18 m^3 Ⓒ 72 m^3

Ⓑ 36 m^3 Ⓓ 192 m^3

14. Which is a right angle?

15. Which is correctly labeled as a line segment?

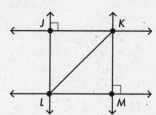

Ⓐ $\overline{JK}$ Ⓒ $\overline{KM}$

Ⓑ $\overline{LM}$ Ⓓ $\overline{KL}$

Reading

PRACTICE 13 • Main Idea and Details

SAMPLES

Directions: Read the passage about workers at the turn of the century. Then answer the questions that follow.

Today, we consider someone who works a 40-hour week a full-time worker. Things were different at the turn of the century. In 1900, the average work week was 59 hours long. That means a person had to work nearly ten hours a day for six days a week. For steelworkers it was even worse. Their bosses expected them to work twelve hours a day.

Workdays were often dangerous as well as long. Miners faced the threat of explosions and cave-ins. Other industrial workers used dangerous equipment. Tens of thousands of workers were hurt on the job each year. Today, work-related injuries are covered by special insurance. But in 1900, injured workers received no help. In fact, if they complained, they were likely to be fired.

A. Which is the best title for this passage?

- Ⓐ "Today's Workers"
- Ⓑ "A Miner's Life in 1900"
- Ⓒ "Working Conditions in the Past"
- Ⓓ "New Jobs of Today"

B. In 1900, how many hours a day did a steelworker have to work?

- Ⓐ six
- Ⓑ eight
- Ⓒ ten
- Ⓓ twelve

Tips and Reminders

- Scan the questions quickly to see what you should look for in the passage.

- Read the whole passage carefully. To find the main idea or main topic, decide what the whole passage is mostly about. To find details, look back at the passage.

Go On →

PRACTICE

Directions: Beads are very popular these days. You can buy beads at a craft or specialty store, or you can make your own. Read these directions for making beads. Then answer questions 1–4.

Start with:
- clay that can be oven-baked; 4 colors (black, white, green, and red)
- a table knife
- wax paper
- toothpick
- thin wire
- a metal baking sheet

Steps:
1. Lay down some wax paper on a table or counter. This will be your work surface.
2. Use the palm of your hand to roll a small piece of white clay into a log. Make the log about as thick as a finger and about five inches long.
3. Roll out narrower strips of red, green, and black. (These strips should be the same length as the white log.)
4. Lay the colored strips lengthwise on top of or beside the white log so that all the strips can be rolled together.
5. Use your hand to roll the new, multicolored log into the width you want your beads to be.
6. With help from an adult, use a table knife to cut through the log every $\frac{1}{2}$ inch. Each chunk is a bead!
7. Use a toothpick to poke a hole through each bead. String the beads on a wire.
8. Place your beads on a cookie sheet. Bake for 10 minutes at 325°F.

1. Which is the best title for this passage?

   Ⓐ "Baking Projects You Can Do"
   Ⓑ "Making Clay Beads"
   Ⓒ "How to Design Jewelry"
   Ⓓ "Having Fun With Crafts"

2. The wire is used to

   Ⓐ cut the clay into beads
   Ⓑ separate the different-colored strips of clay
   Ⓒ create interesting shapes to press into the clay
   Ⓓ string the beads together

3. The thickest piece of clay in each bead should be

   Ⓐ red
   Ⓑ black
   Ⓒ white
   Ⓓ green

4. You should roll out your beads on what kind of surface?

   Ⓐ wax paper
   Ⓑ clay
   Ⓒ cookie sheet
   Ⓓ wire

Go On

Directions: Read this passage about a women's basketball league. Then answer questions 5–8.

At a professional basketball game in 1997, a guard for the New York team was getting ready to enter the game. The player noticed two little girls sitting right next to the court. The player gave one of the girls a high-five and then dashed onto the court.

The player was Rhonda Blades, and she was a member of a brand-new sports league: the Women's National Basketball Association, or W.N.B.A. Although there have been other women's basketball leagues, none has been a huge success. Late in the spring of 1997, commercials for the W.N.B.A. flooded television screens. The W.N.B.A. was determined to fill the stands this time.

Even though many of the players were unknown, families flocked to the games. The tickets were affordable. The games were exciting, and the players were friendly. They were eager to sign autographs and chat with their fans. Things looked bright for the new league.

---

5. Which is the best title for this passage?

(A) "A Special Moment"

(B) "Women in Sports"

(C) "Family Fun"

(D) "A Bright Future"

6. What is this passage mostly about?

(A) a new women's basketball league

(B) the history of women's basketball

(C) two little girls in New York

(D) a player named Rhonda Blades

7. What was one reason why families flocked to W.N.B.A. games?

(A) Women's basketball has always been popular.

(B) The ticket prices were low.

(C) There were many famous players in the league.

(D) Families were invited to join in the games.

8. How did the women in the W.N.B.A. react to their fans in their first season?

(A) They ignored their fans.

(B) They were rude to their fans.

(C) They were friendly to them.

(D) They felt sad about them.

Go On →

Directions: Read the passage about a volcano. Then answer questions 9–12.

> For years, life on the tiny Caribbean island of Montserrat was peaceful and pleasant. Most of the island's roughly 10,000 inhabitants lived at the southern end of the island. Some were farmers. Others ran businesses in the capital city of Plymouth. But in July, 1995, everything changed.
>
> Soufriere Hills, a volcano in the south, began to erupt. Rocks and ash shot into the air. At first islanders were surprised but not frightened. However, in September there was a loud and violent eruption. Terrified villagers fled their houses in the middle of the night.
>
> Since then, the government has forced 5000 people to move away from the dangerous southern end of Montserrat. Nearly 4000 have left the island. Most have gone to other Caribbean islands; some have joined relatives in Britain or the United States. Those who remain live in temporary shelters and try to find work.
>
> The people of Montserrat hope that the volcano will quiet down and life will return to normal. Scientists, however, fear that Soufriere Hills will continue to erupt for years. The future is uncertain.

9. Which is the best title for this passage?

Ⓒ "The Volcano of Montserrat"

Ⓑ "A Tiny Island"

Ⓒ︎ "Life in the Caribbean"

Ⓓ "A Night of Sudden Terror"

10. What happened in July of 1995?

Ⓐ Thousands of citizens fled Montserrat.

Ⓑ Soufriere Hills terrified islanders with a loud and violent eruption.

Ⓒ The government of Montserrat closed parts of the island.

Ⓓ Soufriere Hills began to erupt.

11. After the second eruption, the government forced people to

Ⓐ leave the southern part of the island

Ⓑ move to the United States

Ⓒ stay in their homes

Ⓓ leave their temporary shelters

12. About how many people have left Montserrat since the eruptions began?

Ⓐ 1995

Ⓑ 4000

Ⓒ 5000

Ⓓ 10,000

Stop

Language Arts

PRACTICE 14 • Capitalization

SAMPLES

Directions: Read each passage. Look at the underlined parts. Choose the answer that shows the correct capitalization for each part.

(A)
(B)

> Our neighbor, <u>mr. ramirez</u>, is great. On April 1, he never forgets to play a funny joke on all of us. On <u>the Day before Thanksgiving</u>, he bakes pumpkin pies for the entire neighborhod.

A. Ⓐ Mr. ramirez
   Ⓑ mr. Ramirez
   Ⓒ Mr. Ramirez
   Ⓓ Correct as it is

B. Ⓐ the day before Thanksgiving
   Ⓑ the Day before thanksgiving
   Ⓒ the Day Before Thanksgiving
   Ⓓ Correct as it is

Tips and Reminders

- Check every word that has a capital letter. Decide if the word should be capitalized or not.

- Watch out for words that should be capitalized but are not, such as the names of people and their titles (*Aunt Fay*), the names of places (*Portland, Oregon*), and important words in the titles of published works (*A Tree Grows in Brooklyn*).

PRACTICE

(1)
(2)
(3)

> <u>Edgar allen poe</u> wrote many poems and stories. My favorite poem written by Poe is <u>"the raven."</u> My favorite story is <u>"The Gold Bug."</u>

1. Ⓐ Edgar allen Poe
   Ⓑ edgar allen poe
   Ⓒ Edgar Allen Poe
   Ⓓ Correct as it is

2. Ⓐ "the Raven."
   Ⓑ "The Raven."
   Ⓒ "The raven."
   Ⓓ Correct as it is

3. Ⓐ "The gold bug."
   Ⓑ "The Gold bug."
   Ⓒ "the Gold Bug."
   Ⓓ Correct as it is

Go On →

29 Barn Street
(4)   Ivoryton, connecticut 06442
March 6, 1998

(5)   dear Lindsey,
        Yesterday something funny
happened. We had a substitute
(6)   teacher named ms. Hammond.
When we came into the classroom,
she was reading the lesson plan.
(7)   "What a nice march morning,"
she said. "Your teacher wants me
(8)   to read you a story, "Little Bear's
Birthday."
        She started a tale about a
talking bear. It was kind of cute
but so childish! Then another
substitute knocked on the door.
        "I think we switched lesson
plans and books by mistake," she
(9)   said. "A wrinkle in time is too
difficult for first graders!"
(10)   Your friend,
                       Caitlin

6. Ⓐ Ms. Hammond. when
   Ⓑ ms. hammond. when
   Ⓒ Ms. Hammond. When
   Ⓓ Correct as it is

7. Ⓐ "What a nice March morning,"
      she
   Ⓑ "What a nice March morning,"
      She
   Ⓒ "what a nice March morning,"
      she
   Ⓓ Correct as it is

8. Ⓐ "Little bear's birthday."
   Ⓑ "little bear's birthday."
   Ⓒ "Little Bear's birthday."
   Ⓓ Correct as it is

9. Ⓐ *a wrinkle in time*
   Ⓑ *A Wrinkle in time*
   Ⓒ *A Wrinkle in Time*
   Ⓓ Correct as is

4. Ⓐ Ivoryton, Connecticut
   Ⓑ ivoryton, connnecticut
   Ⓒ ivoryton, Connecticut
   Ⓓ Correct as is

5. Ⓐ dear lindsey
   Ⓑ Dear Lindsey
   Ⓒ Dear lindsey
   Ⓓ Correct as it is

10. Ⓐ Your Friend
    Ⓑ your friend,
    Ⓒ your Friend,
    Ⓓ Correct as it is

Stop

Mathematics

PRACTICE 15 • Measurement

Directions: Choose the best answer to each question.

SAMPLES

A. The play started at 7:30 P.M. and lasted 2 hours 45 minutes. At what time did the play end?

Ⓐ 9:15 P.M.

Ⓑ 9:45 P.M.

Ⓒ 10:00 P.M.

Ⓓ 10:15 P.M.

B. Which unit should be used to measure the weight of a mouse?

Ⓐ kilograms

Ⓑ milligrams

Ⓒ grams

Ⓓ tons

Tips and Reminders

- Use the pictures to find the information you need.

- Make an estimate. Check to see if any of the answer choices is close to your estimate.

- Try each answer choice given. Rule out those that make no sense.

PRACTICE

1. About how high is the door to your classroom?

Ⓐ 6 inches   Ⓒ 6 meters

Ⓑ 6 feet   Ⓓ 6 yards

2. How many seconds are in 12 minutes?

Ⓐ 72 seconds   Ⓒ 240 seconds

Ⓑ 120 seconds   Ⓓ 720 seconds

3. Look at the map and the scale. About how far is it from Camden to Dunston?

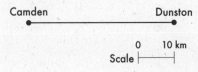

Ⓐ 10 km   Ⓒ 30 km

Ⓑ 20 km   Ⓓ 40 km

Go On →

4. Which unit should be used to measure the distance between your home and the nearest big city?

(A) miles   (C) feet

(B) yards   (D) inches

5. When the train left the station, this was the time on Mara's watch.

The train ride to Philadelphia took 4 hours and 25 minutes. Which watch shows what time Mara arrived in Philadelphia?

(A)   (C)

(B)   (D)

6. Darryl started watching TV at 6:55 P.M. He turned off the TV 1 hour and 10 minutes later. Which clock shows the time he turned off the TV?

(A)   (C)

(B)   (D)

7. How long is the line connecting the two circles? (Use your centimeter ruler.)

(A) 2 cm   (C) 4 cm

(B) 3 cm   (D) 5 cm

8. How long is the toy truck? (Use your inch ruler.)

(A) 2 in.   (C) 3 in.

(B) $2\frac{1}{2}$ in.   (D) $3\frac{1}{2}$ in.

9. 8 meters is equal to how many centimeters?

(A) 0.8 cm

(B) 8 cm

(C) 80 cm

(D) 800 cm

10. 240 ounces is equal to how many pounds?

(A) 8 lb

(B) 12 lb

(C) 15 lb

(D) 24 lb

Go On

11. A family car is closest to which length?

Ⓐ 5–10 ft

Ⓑ 15–20 ft

Ⓒ 30–40 ft

Ⓓ 50–60 ft

12. Which container would be closest to 4 liters in volume?

13. Look at the map and the scale.

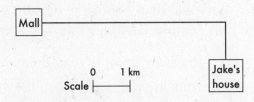

About how far is it from the mall to Jake's house?

Ⓐ 6 km   Ⓒ 8 km

Ⓑ 7 km   Ⓓ 9 km

14. 6 yards is equal to how many feet?

Ⓐ 12 ft

Ⓑ 15 ft

Ⓒ 18 ft

Ⓓ 24 ft

15. Mimi raked leaves from 2:30 P.M. to 4:15 P.M. How long did she rake leaves?

Ⓐ 1 hour 45 minutes

Ⓑ 1 hour 55 minutes

Ⓒ 2 hours 15 minutes

Ⓓ 2 hours 30 minutes

16. Look at the map and the scale.

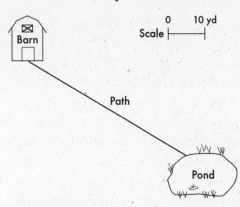

About how far is it along the path from the barn to the closest edge of the pond?

Ⓐ 30 yd

Ⓑ 40 yd

Ⓒ 50 yd

Ⓓ 60 yd

Stop

Reading

PRACTICE 16 • Text Structure

SAMPLES

Directions: Read the passage. Then answer the questions that follow.

If you go to the library and check out a book that was printed 20 years ago, you may see a problem. In many books of that age, the paper is turning yellow and becoming stiff and brittle. Yet, if you looked at a book printed 500 years ago, you would see paper that still looks creamy and soft!

Long ago, paper was made out of linen rags. The paper was expensive but durable. However, in the last century, paper manufacturers began to create their product out of tree pulp. Tree pulp is cheaper than linen, but it contains a substance that turns brown. To make matters even worse, acid was added to the paper. Acid destroys paper eventually. That means many books published in this century will soon fall apart.

Some libraries are copying books onto computers or microfilm. Unfortunately, most books cannot be saved because copying them is so expensive.

A. Which event happened first?

- Ⓐ Books were copied on microfilm.
- Ⓑ Books were printed on rag paper.
- Ⓒ Books began turning brown.
- Ⓓ Paper was made out of trees.

B. How is 500-year-old paper different from paper made in the last century?

- Ⓐ It lasts longer.
- Ⓑ It turns yellow.
- Ⓒ It falls apart.
- Ⓓ It is cheaper to buy.

C. Why will many books published in this century fall apart soon?

- Ⓐ Too many people read them.
- Ⓑ They are damaged when they are copied onto computer or microfilm.
- Ⓒ They are made out of old rags.
- Ⓓ They contain acid that destroys paper.

Tips and Reminders • Look for signal words in the passage. For example, to find the sequence of events, look for dates or for words such as *first, then, later, next.*

Go On

PRACTICE

Directions: Read each passage. Then answer the questions that follow.

Emily was due at her swimming lesson at 4:15. She packed her swimsuit, towel, and hair dryer. Then she grabbed a snack and hopped in the car. She and her mother always did errands on their way to the pool.

First they stopped at the dry cleaner's.

"Phew!" exclaimed Emily's mom. "They got that ink stain out of your one good dress!"

"Too bad," sighed Emily.

Then they were on their way to the pet store for dog biscuits for their puppy. Mrs. Burke groaned because the car was overheating.

Luckily, they were only a short distance from Art's Service Station. However, at 4:30 they were still sitting in the station. Art was working on the car. Emily and her mother were passing the time by eating apple turnovers from the bakery across the street and playing "20 Questions."

---

1. What did Emily do just after she packed her swim bag?

   Ⓐ She went to her lesson.

   Ⓑ She ate cookies from a bakery.

   Ⓒ She stained her good dress.

   Ⓓ She grabbed a snack.

2. Why did Mrs. Burke groan?

   Ⓐ She was having car problems.

   Ⓑ She had forgotten the dog biscuits.

   Ⓒ Her daughter had stained her dress.

   Ⓓ She was near a service station.

3. How was Emily's afternoon different from what she expected?

   Ⓐ She had to pack her bag.

   Ⓑ She went to a party and played a game.

   Ⓒ She was at a service station instead of at the pool.

   Ⓓ She did errands with her mother.

4. Which errand did Emily and Mrs. Burke do first?

   Ⓐ They went to the pool.

   Ⓑ They went to the service station.

   Ⓒ They went to the pet store.

   Ⓓ They went to the dry cleaner's.

Go On

In 1997, the number of Dalmatians dropped off at animal shelters rose dramatically. Why were so many people abandoning these spotted dogs?

In 1996, a new version of the children's movie *101 Dalmatians* was released. Animal rights experts and the movie makers warned viewers not to get carried away and buy a pet dog without carefully considering the responsibility. Still, many parents rushed out to buy their kids a Dalmatian as soon as they saw the movie.

The dogs in the film were cuddly and adorable. However, real Dalmatians aren't always so cute. They sometimes bite, and they get along with adults better than with children. Some new owners ended up disliking their pets, and so they got rid of them. Animal rescue groups struggled to find new homes for the pets.

5. Why did so many people buy Dalmatians in 1996?

Ⓐ Animal rescue groups offered them for sale.

Ⓑ People wanted their dogs to be in a movie about Dalmatians.

Ⓒ Movie makers urged everyone to buy a Dalmatian.

Ⓓ Parents wanted their kids to have a pet like the ones in *101 Dalmatians*.

6. Why did so many of the Dalmatians end up in animal shelters?

Ⓐ Their owners didn't like them.

Ⓑ Their owners couldn't afford to feed them.

Ⓒ The dogs ran away.

Ⓓ Animal rights experts rescued them from cruel owners.

7. Which event happened last?

Ⓐ Animal rescue groups found homes for Dalmatians.

Ⓑ Parents bought Dalmatians.

Ⓒ *101 Dalmatians* was released.

Ⓓ People got rid of their pet Dalmatians.

8. How are real Dalmatians different from the dogs in the movie?

Ⓐ The real dogs are cuter.

Ⓑ The real dogs don't get along with adults.

Ⓒ The real dogs aren't spotted.

Ⓓ The real dogs sometimes bite.

Go On

One moment Maud was on the swings, but the next moment she was flat on the ground spitting sand out of her mouth.

She had just swung up high when her friends Jody and Christine dashed by on their way to the playscape. She had leaned way forward to yell hi, lost her balance, and slipped off the swing. She had landed on her left hand and then fallen onto her face. Mr. Luca, the teacher on playground duty, helped her up and led her to the nurse's office.

The nurse inspected Maud's left hand.

"I don't see any cuts, bruises, or swelling," she said. "But I'm worried that you can't bend your left ring finger."

Maud's dad picked her up and drove her to the clinic, where the doctor ordered an X-ray.

"Yep, it's broken," announced the doctor cheerfully. "Fortunately, it's just a little fracture. I'll put a splint on it, and we'll look at it again in a week."

9. How did Maud break her finger?

ⓐ She fell off a swing.

ⓑ Her friends bumped her as they ran by.

ⓒ She fell off the slide at the playground.

ⓓ She slipped on a patch of sand.

10. What happened just after Maud fell to the ground?

ⓐ Her dad picked her up.

ⓑ Her friends dashed by.

ⓒ She went to the nurse's office.

ⓓ Mr. Luca helped her up.

11. What happened just before the doctor announced that the finger was broken?

ⓐ Maud's dad drove her to the clinic.

ⓑ The nurse worried about one finger.

ⓒ The doctor ordered an X-ray.

ⓓ The nurse put a splint on the finger.

12. How was the broken finger different from the other fingers?

ⓐ It could not bend.

ⓑ It was swollen.

ⓒ It had a cut on it.

ⓓ It was bruised.

Stop

Language Arts

PRACTICE 17 • Spelling

SAMPLES

Directions: Read each sentence. If one of the underlined words is misspelled, fill in the bubble under that word. If all of the words are spelled correctly, fill in the bubble under answer D, "No mistake."

A. The <u>student</u> walked up and down the <u>aisles</u> <u>collecting</u> papers. <u>No mistake</u>
    Ⓐ   Ⓑ   Ⓒ   Ⓓ

B. My <u>stomich</u> felt <u>awful</u> after I <u>gobbled</u> ten pancakes. <u>No mistake</u>
    Ⓐ   Ⓑ   Ⓒ   Ⓓ

> **Tips and Reminders**
>
> - Eliminate any answer choices that you know are spelled correctly.
>
> - Apply the spelling rules that you know, such as "*i* before *e* except after *c*, or when sounding like *a* as in *neighbor* and *weigh*."
>
> - If you are not sure which word is misspelled, look for an answer choice that looks wrong or that you have never seen before.

PRACTICE

1. Jack <u>labelled</u> the <u>envelopes</u> and <u>separated</u> them into neat piles. <u>No mistake</u>
      Ⓐ   Ⓑ   Ⓒ   Ⓓ

2. Mom <u>repeated</u> her <u>instructions</u> about being <u>carefull</u> when biking. <u>No mistake</u>
       Ⓐ   Ⓑ   Ⓒ   Ⓓ

3. We were <u>uncertain</u> whether it was <u>necesary</u> to call the <u>plumber</u>. <u>No mistake</u>
         Ⓐ   Ⓑ   Ⓒ   Ⓓ

4. It is <u>irresponsible</u> to buy a horse unless you are <u>equiped</u> to <u>maintain</u> it. <u>No mistake</u>
      Ⓐ   Ⓑ   Ⓒ   Ⓓ

Go On →

5. The <u>poster</u> showed the two <u>heroes</u> chasing a <u>gostly</u> creature. <u>No mistake</u>
Ⓐ   Ⓑ   Ⓒ   Ⓓ

6. I am <u>sincerly</u> <u>pleased</u> to make your <u>acquaintance</u>. <u>No mistake</u>
   Ⓐ   Ⓑ   Ⓒ   Ⓓ

7. To reach the <u>cellar</u>, you must <u>descend</u> some very <u>crooked</u> stairs. <u>No mistake</u>
       Ⓐ   Ⓑ   Ⓒ   Ⓓ

8. The class read a <u>magazine</u> <u>article</u> about dolphins and <u>porpoises</u>. <u>No mistake</u>
        Ⓐ   Ⓑ   Ⓒ   Ⓓ

9. We had an <u>arguement</u> about when the <u>blizzard</u> <u>occurred</u>. <u>No mistake</u>
       Ⓐ   Ⓑ   Ⓒ   Ⓓ

10. Lianna has an <u>extrordinary</u> <u>opportunity</u> to <u>travel</u> in Mexico. <u>No mistake</u>
      Ⓐ   Ⓑ   Ⓒ   Ⓓ

11. <u>Beautiful</u> red <u>tomatoes</u> <u>glissened</u> on the vines. <u>No mistake</u>
   Ⓐ   Ⓑ   Ⓒ   Ⓓ

12. Would you be <u>embarassed</u> to <u>receive</u> the <u>award</u>? <u>No mistake</u>
     Ⓐ   Ⓑ   Ⓒ   Ⓓ

13. Our teacher <u>explaned</u> the <u>directions</u> <u>several</u> times. <u>No mistake</u>
     Ⓐ   Ⓑ   Ⓒ   Ⓓ

14. The <u>naughty</u> baby took all of the <u>bowls</u> out of the <u>cupboard</u>. <u>No mistake</u>
   Ⓐ   Ⓑ   Ⓒ   Ⓓ

15. Calvin <u>howled</u> as the bats <u>cercled</u> over our <u>heads</u>. <u>No mistake</u>
   Ⓐ   Ⓑ   Ⓒ   Ⓓ

Stop →

Mathematics

PRACTICE 18 • Computation

Directions: Find the answer to each problem. If the correct answer is not given, fill in the bubble for N, "Not Given."

SAMPLES

A.   154
   $+ 17$

Ⓐ 161
Ⓑ 163
Ⓒ 171
Ⓓ N

B. 6)272

Ⓐ 45 R2
Ⓑ 46
Ⓒ 46 R4
Ⓓ N

C. $\frac{1}{6} + \frac{3}{6} =$

Ⓐ $\frac{2}{3}$
Ⓑ $\frac{4}{12}$
Ⓒ $\frac{5}{6}$
Ⓓ N

D. $6.8 - 0.4 =$

Ⓐ 7.2
Ⓑ 6.6
Ⓒ 6.2
Ⓓ N

Tips and Reminders

• Look at the sign to see if you need to add (+), subtract (–), multiply (×), or divide (÷ or ⌐).

• Always check your answer.

• When you add or subtract fractions, be sure to simplify your answer. For example, in sample C, $\frac{1}{6} + \frac{3}{6} = \frac{4}{6}$, which can be simplified to $\frac{2}{3}$.

• When using decimal numbers, make sure you line up the decimal points before you add or subtract.

PRACTICE

1.   234
   $- 199$

Ⓐ 33
Ⓑ 35
Ⓒ 45
Ⓓ N

2.   277
   $+ 694$

Ⓐ 971
Ⓑ 961
Ⓒ 871
Ⓓ N

Go On

3. $74 \div 8 =$
- Ⓐ 8 R10
- Ⓑ 9
- Ⓒ 9 R2
- Ⓓ N

4. $17 \times 15 =$
- Ⓐ 155
- Ⓑ 245
- Ⓒ 255
- Ⓓ N

5. $5421 - 3963 =$
- Ⓐ 1468
- Ⓑ 1458
- Ⓒ 1452
- Ⓓ N

6. $300 \times 12 =$
- Ⓐ 36
- Ⓑ 360
- Ⓒ 3600
- Ⓓ N

7. $581 \div 14 =$
- Ⓐ 40 R7
- Ⓑ 40 R9
- Ⓒ 42 R4
- Ⓓ N

8. $63 \times 77 =$
- Ⓐ 882
- Ⓑ 4631
- Ⓒ 4851
- Ⓓ N

9. $3600 \div 6 =$
- Ⓐ 6
- Ⓑ 60
- Ⓒ 600
- Ⓓ N

10. $975 - 586 =$
- Ⓐ 499
- Ⓑ 399
- Ⓒ 299
- Ⓓ N

11. $2.7 + 8.9 =$
- Ⓐ 10.6
- Ⓑ 11.15
- Ⓒ 11.6
- Ⓓ N

12. $7\overline{)364}$
- Ⓐ 52
- Ⓑ 62
- Ⓒ 520
- Ⓓ N

13. $\frac{2}{5} + \frac{1}{5} =$
- Ⓐ $\frac{2}{10}$
- Ⓑ $\frac{3}{5}$
- Ⓒ $\frac{3}{25}$
- Ⓓ N

14. $\$6.70 + \$3.50 =$
- Ⓐ $10.20
- Ⓑ $9.30
- Ⓒ $9.20
- Ⓓ N

Go On

15. $\frac{5}{6} - \frac{1}{2} =$

    Ⓐ $\frac{1}{3}$

    Ⓑ $\frac{3}{6}$

    Ⓒ $\frac{3}{12}$

    Ⓓ N

16. $\frac{3}{4} + \frac{2}{8} =$

    Ⓐ $\frac{5}{12}$

    Ⓑ $\frac{6}{32}$

    Ⓒ 1

    Ⓓ N

17. $\begin{array}{r} \$23.95 \\ -\,18.67 \\ \hline \end{array}$

    Ⓐ $15.28

    Ⓑ $5.38

    Ⓒ $5.28

    Ⓓ N

18. $66 \div 7 =$

    Ⓐ 9

    Ⓑ 9 R3

    Ⓒ 10 R4

    Ⓓ N

19. $20 \times 83 =$

    Ⓐ 160

    Ⓑ 166

    Ⓒ 16,600

    Ⓓ N

20. $3.5 - 1.9 =$

    Ⓐ 0.6

    Ⓑ 1.6

    Ⓒ 2.6

    Ⓓ N

21. $\begin{array}{r} 8253 \\ +\,5641 \\ \hline \end{array}$

    Ⓐ 13,894

    Ⓑ 14,894

    Ⓒ 24,494

    Ⓓ N

22. $18\overline{)432}$

    Ⓐ 16 R2

    Ⓑ 23

    Ⓒ 24

    Ⓓ N

23. $203 \times 5 =$

    Ⓐ 1005

    Ⓑ 1015

    Ⓒ 1150

    Ⓓ N

24. $\frac{6}{12} + \frac{3}{12} =$

    Ⓐ $\frac{9}{24}$

    Ⓑ $\frac{2}{3}$

    Ⓒ $\frac{3}{12}$

    Ⓓ N

25. $\begin{array}{r} 31 \\ 228 \\ +\,45 \\ \hline \end{array}$

    Ⓐ 304

    Ⓑ 303

    Ⓒ 294

    Ⓓ N

26. $\$3.25 \times 6 =$

    Ⓐ $19.50

    Ⓑ $19.20

    Ⓒ $18.50

    Ⓓ N

Stop

Reading

PRACTICE 19 • Inferences

SAMPLES

Directions: Read the passage. Then answer the questions that follow.

Lyle pushed his mashed potatoes into a peak. "It looks like a snow-covered mountain, like the ones we could see from our old house," he said.

His sister glared at him. "For the last time, Lyle, stop talking about the old house!" she demanded. "This is our home now."

Lyle looked out the window. The green grass was all wrong for December, and the flatness of the land was wrong, too. This would never feel like home.

A. What can you tell about the place where Lyle lives now?

(A) It is in the mountains.

(B) It has warm winters.

(C) It is a large city.

(D) It has friendly people.

B. How is Lyle's sister feeling toward him?

(A) understanding and kind

(B) surprised and confused

(C) impatient and annoyed

(D) sad and worried

Tips and Reminders

- To draw conclusions or make predictions, look for clues in the passage.

- Check each answer choice to decide which is most likely.

Go On

Directions: Read this passage about Rosie and her father. Then answer questions 1–4.

Rosie grabbed a package of hot dogs and held them up to Dad. He shook his head. "Find the low-fat hot dogs with the green label," he said.

In the next aisle, Rosie picked out a bottle of Orchard Fruit Drink. Again, Dad shook his head. "Not enough vitamin C in that brand," he said. "It's mostly water, sugar, and flavoring."

In the third aisle, Rosie grabbed a bag of salted cheese tortilla strips and held them up. Dad just shook his head.

Dad glanced at his shopping list. "Okay," he said to Rosie. "Now we need to find some things for your school snack."

1. Where does this story take place?

Ⓐ in a supermarket

Ⓑ in a school lunchroom

Ⓒ in a restaurant

Ⓓ in a kitchen

2. What kind of food will Dad probably let Rosie buy for her school snack?

Ⓐ cookies

Ⓑ pudding

Ⓒ chips

Ⓓ fruit

3. What can you tell about the hot dogs Rosie held up to Dad?

Ⓐ They are the best-selling brand.

Ⓑ They contain a lot of fat.

Ⓒ They make a good snack.

Ⓓ They do not have any vitamin C.

4. When Dad chooses food, he is most concerned about

Ⓐ how much it costs

Ⓑ how tasty it is

Ⓒ how much Rosie likes it

Ⓓ how healthful it is

Go On

Directions: Read this passage about what happened to three famous artists. Then answer questions 5–8.

What happens when an artist goes blind? French painter Claude Monet faced this problem in his old age, but he would not stop painting. He just changed his style. He began painting with large, loose strokes. The paintings he did this way are some of his best.

Ludwig van Beethoven is one of the greatest musical composers of all time. He began to go deaf as a young man. But he could "hear" musical ideas in his head. So he just kept on writing wonderful music.

By age 20, Tanaquil LeClercq was a famous ballerina. Then she fell ill with polio and nearly died. Although doctors saved her life, she could never dance again. Still, LeClercq could not give up the world of ballet. From her wheelchair, she taught other young women to dance as gracefully as she once did.

5. This passage about what happened to three different artists suggests that

   Ⓐ painters, composers, and dancers are usually successful

   Ⓑ people can find ways to overcome physical problems

   Ⓒ people should never change their careers

   Ⓓ famous and talented people have terrible luck

6. From reading this passage, what can you tell about how Monet painted before he went blind?

   Ⓐ He used small, tight strokes.

   Ⓑ He painted mostly people.

   Ⓒ He used dark, quiet colors.

   Ⓓ He made very large paintings.

7. What happened to Tanaquil LeClercq when she fell ill with polio?

   Ⓐ She lost her hearing.

   Ⓑ She was unable to talk to others.

   Ⓒ She started to go blind.

   Ⓓ She lost the use of her legs.

8. What did Monet, Beethoven, and LeClercq have in common?

   Ⓐ They loved their work.

   Ⓑ They had illnesses that nearly killed them.

   Ⓒ They wanted to be famous.

   Ⓓ They felt sorry for themselves because of their problems.

Go On

Directions: This story is about a dog who shows up on a boy's doorstep. Read the story and then answer questions 9–12.

The stray dog had been with us for two weeks. He wasn't much to look at, but a bath and brushing had helped. He still had doggy breath, though. We named him Dragon. "Just something to call him until his owner claims him," Mom and I had said.

We had put up posters all over the neighborhood, but no one ever called. Now Mom was reading the "Lost Pet" ads, as she had each day since Dragon showed up. When she finished, she sighed and said, "Let's face it, son. No one's looking for Dragon."

"Do we take him to the animal shelter?" I asked.

"We could," Mom began, "or I could increase your allowance so you could afford to buy dog food."

I thought for a minute. Dragon was not the dog I would have picked out for myself. But he was okay, and he needed a home.

9. Why did the boy and his mother name the dog Dragon?

Ⓐ He was very large.

Ⓑ He was unfriendly.

Ⓒ He had smelly breath.

Ⓓ He had a scary bark.

10. The "Lost Pet" ads that the boy's mother read were probably

Ⓐ on a poster

Ⓑ in a letter

Ⓒ in a magazine

Ⓓ in the newspaper

11. How did the boy and his mother feel about Dragon at the end of the story?

Ⓐ They were starting to like him.

Ⓑ They thought he was terrific.

Ⓒ They were afraid of him.

Ⓓ They thought he was a pest.

12. What do you think the boy will do next?

Ⓐ take Dragon to the animal shelter

Ⓑ put up more posters around the neighborhood

Ⓒ tell his mother he wants to keep Dragon

Ⓓ spend his allowance on something special for himself

Go On

Directions: Read this passage about what people do at baseball games. Then answer questions 13–16.

Have you ever been to a professional baseball game? If you have, you know what happens in the middle of the seventh inning. Everyone stands up and stretches. Then they sit back down again.

The first "seventh-inning stretch" happened more than 80 years ago at a game attended by President William Howard Taft. President Taft, who was six feet tall, weighed over 300 pounds. By the time the seventh inning rolled around, he felt the need to get up from his seat. Many people saw the President get to his feet. Thinking he was leaving, they stood up. Then Taft sat back down, so the crowd did, too.

Why has this funny tradition continued? Baseball games usually last at least three hours, and ballpark seats are hard and narrow. Most fans agree that the seventh-inning stretch makes good sense.

13. What can you be sure will happen if you go to a professional baseball game?

   Ⓐ The game will last three hours.

   Ⓑ The President will attend the game.

   Ⓒ You will find a comfortable seat.

   Ⓓ Fans will get up and stretch during the seventh inning.

14. Why did many people stand when President Taft got up?

   Ⓐ They were showing respect for him.

   Ⓑ They were getting ready to leave the ballpark.

   Ⓒ They wanted to get a good look at him.

   Ⓓ They wanted to buy refreshments.

15. What can you tell about President Taft from reading this passage?

   Ⓐ He had a favorite baseball team.

   Ⓑ He was a very large man.

   Ⓒ He was an excellent president.

   Ⓓ He enjoyed many sports.

16. How do most baseball fans probably start to feel by the seventh inning?

   Ⓐ bored and impatient

   Ⓑ nervous and worried

   Ⓒ cramped and uncomfortable

   Ⓓ hungry and tired

Language Arts

PRACTICE 20 • Combining Sentences

SAMPLES

Directions: Read the two sentences in the box. Choose the best way to combine them to form one sentence.

> **A.** Liza borrowed a knapsack.
> She borrowed it from Mark.

Ⓐ Liza borrowed a knapsack, she borrowed it from Mark.

Ⓑ Liza borrowed a knapsack, and she borrowed it from Mark.

Ⓒ Liza borrowed a knapsack, but she borrowed it from Mark.

Ⓓ Liza borrowed a knapsack from Mark.

Directions: Read the passage and answer the question that follows.

Frank wanted to find a summer job. He applied for a job at the grocery store, but he was too young. Eventually, he found a job. Frank baby-sits for Abby Stein. He baby-sits for Tyler Ramsey.

B. Which is the best way to combine the last two sentences?

Ⓐ Frank baby-sits for Abby Stein and Tyler Ramsey.

Ⓑ Frank baby-sits for Abby Stein and baby-sits for Tyler Ramsey.

Ⓒ Frank baby-sits for Abby Stein but for Tyler Ramsey, too.

Ⓓ Frank baby-sits for Abby Stein, Frank baby-sits for Tyler Ramsey.

Tips and Reminders

- Check the order of words in the combined sentence to make sure it is correct.

- Make sure the combined sentence has the same meaning as the two original sentences.

- Be careful in using conjunctions and connecting words, such as *and, but, so,* and *although.* Using an incorrect conjunction can change the meaning of the sentence.

Go On

PRACTICE

Directions: Read the two sentences in the box. Choose the best way to combine them to form one sentence.

1. | Hanna enjoys movies like this one.
   This movie is scary.

   Ⓐ Hanna enjoys movies like this scary movie.

   Ⓑ This movie is scary like Hanna enjoys.

   Ⓒ Hanna enjoys scary movies like this one.

   Ⓓ Movies Hanna enjoys are scary like this one.

2. | Papa speaks Spanish and English.
   I have learned both languages.

   Ⓐ I have learned both languages and Papa speaks Spanish and English.

   Ⓑ Papa speaks Spanish and English, so I have learned both languages.

   Ⓒ I have learned Spanish and English and both languages Papa speaks.

   Ⓓ Papa speaks Spanish and English, but I have learned both languages.

3. | Parents built the new playground.
   Children built the new playground.

   Ⓐ Parents and children built the new playground.

   Ⓑ Parents built the new playground, and children, too.

   Ⓒ Parents built the playground, children built the new playground.

   Ⓓ Parents built the new playground, but so did children.

4. | Lin is a talented musician.
   She can play four instruments.

   Ⓐ She can play four instruments, Lin is a talented musician.

   Ⓑ Lin is a talented musician, but she can play four instruments.

   Ⓒ She can play four instruments, Lin, a talented musician.

   Ⓓ Lin, a talented musician, can play four instruments.

5. | We called a tow truck.
   Our car broke down.

   Ⓐ We called a tow truck, and our car broke down.

   Ⓑ Our car broke down, we called a tow truck.

   Ⓒ We called a tow truck because our car broke down.

   Ⓓ Our car broke down, but we called a tow truck.

6. | Les wrote an interesting article.
   He wrote it for the school newspaper.

   Ⓐ Les wrote an article for the school newspaper, and it was interesting.

   Ⓑ Les wrote an interesting article for the school newspaper.

   Ⓒ Les wrote an interesting article, he wrote it for the school newspaper.

   Ⓓ Les wrote an article, it was interesting, for the school newspaper.

Go On →

Directions: Read each passage and answer the questions that follow.

> Isn't it interesting about names? Some people's names match their addresses. I know a woman named Roberta Mains who lives on Main Street. A family named Flowers lives on Rose Lane. John Gray III lives in a gray house. He lives on Third Avenue.

7. Which is the best way to combine the first two sentences?

Ⓐ Isn't it interesting that some people's names match their addresses?

Ⓑ Isn't it interesting about some people and their addresses?

Ⓒ Isn't it interesting about names and addresses that match?

Ⓓ Isn't it interesting about names and about addresses that some match?

8. Which is the best way to combine the last two sentences?

Ⓐ John Gray III lives in a gray house, so he lives on Third Avenue.

Ⓑ John Gray III lives in a gray house, he lives on Third Avenue.

Ⓒ John Gray III lives in a gray house but on Third Avenue.

Ⓓ John Gray III lives in a gray house on Third Avenue.

> The carpenter measured the boards. She cut the boards. Then she checked everything again before she started to build. She was ready. She began nailing the boards on the frame.

9. Which is the best way to combine the first two sentences?

Ⓐ The carpenter measured the boards and cut the boards.

Ⓑ The boards the carpenter cut she measured.

Ⓒ The carpenter measured and cut the boards.

Ⓓ The boards, they were measured by the carpenter and cut.

10. Which is the best way to combine the last two sentences?

Ⓐ When she was ready, she began nailing the boards on the frame.

Ⓑ She was ready as she began nailing the boards on the frame.

Ⓒ Although she was ready, she began nailing the boards.

Ⓓ She was ready, she began nailing the boards on the frame.

Stop

Mathematics

PRACTICE 21 • Estimation

Directions: Choose the best answer to each question.

SAMPLES

A. The closest estimate of $103 + 88$ is —

  Ⓐ 170

  Ⓑ 180

  Ⓒ 190

  Ⓓ 200

B. 22×19 is between —

  Ⓐ 250 and 300

  Ⓑ 300 and 350

  Ⓒ 350 and 400

  Ⓓ 400 and 450

Tips and Reminders

• Use rounding to estimate.

• Use number sense to check your answer.

PRACTICE

1. The closest estimate of $391 - 197$ is —

  Ⓐ 100

  Ⓑ 200

  Ⓒ 300

  Ⓓ 400

2. The closest estimate of $6280 \div 9$ is —

  Ⓐ 7

  Ⓑ 70

  Ⓒ 700

  Ⓓ 7000

3. Which numbers should be used to estimate $807.95 + $48.85?

  Ⓐ $800 + $50

  Ⓑ $800 + $40

  Ⓒ $850 + $50

  Ⓓ $850 + $40

4. Which is the closest estimate of 6×145?

  Ⓐ 60

  Ⓑ 90

  Ⓒ 600

  Ⓓ 900

Go On

6 ft

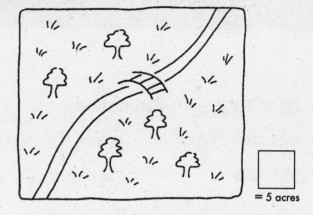

= 5 acres

5. Which is the closest estimate of the length of this train car?

Ⓐ 40 ft

Ⓑ 60 ft

Ⓒ 80 ft

Ⓓ 100 ft

6. 539 ÷ 9 is —

Ⓐ less than 40

Ⓑ between 40 and 50

Ⓒ between 50 and 60

Ⓓ more than 60

7. Which numbers should be used to estimate 3057 + 14,950?

Ⓐ 3000 + 15,000

Ⓑ 3000 + 20,000

Ⓒ 4000 + 15,000

Ⓓ 4000 + 20,000

8. One paperback book costs $6.95. Which is the closest estimate of the cost of 8 books?

Ⓐ $70

Ⓑ $65

Ⓒ $60

Ⓓ $56

9. Which is the best estimate of the total number of acres in the park?

Ⓐ 50

Ⓑ 100

Ⓒ 150

Ⓓ 200

10. 5419 – 2980 is —

Ⓐ less than 2000

Ⓑ between 2000 and 2500

Ⓒ between 2500 and 3000

Ⓓ more than 3000

11. 41,677 ÷ 7 is closest to —

Ⓐ 60

Ⓑ 600

Ⓒ 6000

Ⓓ 60,000

12. Nobuo earned $57, $82, and $39. Which numbers should be used to estimate how much he earned in all?

Ⓐ $60 + $80 + $40

Ⓑ $50 + $80 + $40

Ⓒ $60 + $90 + $40

Ⓓ $50 + $90 + $30

Stop

Reading

PRACTICE 22 • Literary Elements

Directions: Read the passage. Then answer the questions that follow.

SAMPLES

Kurt stood at the edge of the dock. If he waited much longer, the other boys would notice his fear. But Kurt could not shake off his awful memory.

Last summer he had been swimming in this same pond. After diving from the dock, he had caught his foot in the weeds at the bottom and could not get himself loose. All he could think of was the feeling he had experienced as he gasped and choked in the deep green water—before his brother rescued him.

"Come on, Kurt! The water's great!" shouted one of the boys.

The next instant, Kurt leaped into the air and pulled his knees to his chest. Then he waited to hear the sound of his body splashing into the water.

A. How does Kurt feel as he stands on the dock?

   Ⓐ bold

   Ⓑ excited

   Ⓒ fearful

   Ⓓ curious

B. What is Kurt's problem in this story?

   Ⓐ He thinks it is too cold for swimming.

   Ⓑ He remembers a time he nearly drowned.

   Ⓒ He is not allowed to go swimming.

   Ⓓ His friends will not go in the water with him.

Tips and Reminders

- Look back at the passage to answer questions about details.

- For other questions, you may need to "read between the lines." Think about the story and what you already know to answer these questions.

Go On

PRACTICE

Directions: Read this story about what happens to two brothers. Then answer questions 1–4.

Two rich brothers were walking down the road when they came upon an old man dressed in tattered clothes. "Could you spare just one silver coin?" the old man asked the brothers.

The first brother walked past the old man. "A man gets rich by working for his money," he told the beggar impatiently.

The second brother took a bag of silver coins from his coat pocket. Handing it to the old man, he said kindly, "Buy all the clothes and food you need."

Then the two brothers set off down the road again. When they had walked nearly a mile, they were overtaken by a band of thieves. The thieves took a bag of silver coins from the first brother. Then they searched the second brother. When they realized that he had nothing for them to steal, they ran off with their bag of coins, laughing with delight.

1. What lesson can be learned from this story?

   Ⓐ Work hard to earn your own way.

   Ⓑ It is foolish to save your money.

   Ⓒ Be kind to those who are in need.

   Ⓓ Great wealth makes people happy.

2. Which word best describes the first brother?

   Ⓐ selfish

   Ⓑ shrewd

   Ⓒ stubborn

   Ⓓ careful

3. When they discovered that the second brother had no coins, the thieves

   Ⓐ pushed him to the ground

   Ⓑ said they would rob him later

   Ⓒ ran away laughing

   Ⓓ took his coat from him

4. What kind of story is this?

   Ⓐ science fiction

   Ⓑ myth

   Ⓒ biography

   Ⓓ folk tale

Go On

Directions: This story is about a girl who stands up for what she believes in. Read the story to find out what happens. Then answer questions 5–8.

Lynn had been standing in the crowd in front of the Tate Building all morning. A light rain had started falling, and it was washing away the lettering of her home-made sign. "SAVE THE TATE BUILDING," the sign had said.

As far as Lynn was concerned, the Tate Building was the finest structure in the whole downtown area. Sure, it was much older than the other buildings around it, but it was beautiful. Lynn did not want to see it destroyed to make way for a square modern building with no history and no character.

A groan went up from the crowd. A worker had started the motor of the wrecking vehicle. Now he was driving it slowly toward the Tate Building. In a few moments, the wrecking ball would crash against the old brick wall.

Lynn rolled up her soggy sign. As she pushed it into a trash can, she made herself a promise. She would never eat at the restaurant that was going to be built where the Tate Building had stood for 150 years.

5. Where does this story take place?

(A) in a restaurant

(B) at a parking garage

(C) outside an old building

(D) at Lynn's home

6. What is the mood of this story?

(A) nervous

(B) sad

(C) frightened

(D) bored

7. What is the main problem in this story?

(A) The rain is ruining Lynn's sign.

(B) Lynn does not like eating in restaurants.

(C) A worker is late for his job.

(D) The Tate Building is being torn down.

8. What kind of story is this?

(A) a legend

(B) realistic fiction

(C) a fable

(D) science fiction

Directions: Read this story about what happens to a boy named Terry. Then answer questions 9–12.

Mom eased the car into a space in the library parking lot. "Okay, Terry. We're here ten minutes early, just as I promised," she said.

Terry got out of the car and looked around at the other band members gathering for the Fourth of July parade. Most of them seemed relaxed, but not Terry. This was his first parade, and he had gotten up at dawn to make sure everything would be just right. He had polished his flute and ironed every wrinkle out of his uniform. He had practiced his music until he played it perfectly.

Mom gave Terry a kiss for good luck. "You'll hear me cheering when you come down Main Street," she said. Then she got into her car and pulled away.

Terry waved until the car was out of sight. Then he remembered. His flute was still in the trunk of Mom's car.

9. What lesson can be learned from this story?

   Ⓐ Careful planning does not always prevent problems.

   Ⓑ Never wish anyone good luck.

   Ⓒ Practicing is usually a waste of time.

   Ⓓ Try to be an early riser.

10. What kind of person is Terry?

   Ⓐ He doesn't care if other people like him.

   Ⓑ He likes to have fun.

   Ⓒ He expects other people to help him.

   Ⓓ He wants to do his best.

11. What did Terry forget to do?

   Ⓐ iron his uniform

   Ⓑ get his flute out of the car

   Ⓒ learn his music

   Ⓓ leave early for the parade

12. What is the mood at the beginning of this story?

   Ⓐ excited and nervous

   Ⓑ surprised and bothered

   Ⓒ happy and calm

   Ⓓ embarrassed and afraid

Stop

Language Arts

PRACTICE 23 • Composition

SAMPLES

Directions: Read the passage below. Then answer the questions that follow.

Rubén Darío

Darío was born in 1867 in Nicaragua. He disliked the old style of
 (1)   (2)
Spanish poetry, so he created a new style. His poems were modern and
                                                    (3)
elegant. Other Hispanic poets noticed and tried to write as Darío did.
         (4)
In this way, Rubén Darío brought great changes to Spanish poetry.
 (5)

A. Which sentence would best fit at the beginning of this passage before sentence 1?

Ⓐ Some people make a living by writing poetry.

Ⓑ The poems of Rubén Darío are widely admired.

Ⓒ His best work is *Songs of Life and Hope.*

Ⓓ Rubén Darío traveled abroad.

B. The author probably wrote this passage to –

Ⓐ encourage people to read poems

Ⓑ describe the country of Nicaragua

Ⓒ tell about a famous poet

Ⓓ make people like modern poetry

Tips and Reminders

• The topic sentence should tell what the whole paragraph is mostly about. Every sentence in that paragraph should support, or be about, that topic.

• To determine the author's purpose, think about what the author is trying to say.

Go On

PRACTICE

No Messages

The telephone answering machine is a bad idea. This invention is
(1)   (2)
intended to make life simpler, but it doesn't. When you come home
(3)
from a long day at work or school, you have to check the machine and

call back the people who called you. You have to call them back, and
(4)
that's because your message told them you would. Now think about it.
(5)
Wouldn't it be nicer just to sit down and relax—at least until the
(6)
telephone rings?

---

1. The author probably wrote this passage to —

(A) persuade people to call their friends more often

(B) explain how to use an anwering machine

(C) compare good and bad inventions

(D) convince people not to use answering machines

2. How would sentence 4 best be revised without changing its meaning?

(A) You have to call them back because your message told them you would.

(B) Your message told them, so you have to call them back.

(C) Your message, it told them you would call them back, so you have to call them.

(D) You call them back because you have to, as your message said.

3. Which sentence could be added before sentence 6?

(A) A ringing telephone is a bother.

(B) Are any of your calls really that important?

(C) Some people leave messages that are hard to understand.

(D) Does your answering machine ever break down?

4. What is the topic sentence of this paragraph?

(A) sentence 1

(B) sentence 3

(C) sentence 4

(D) sentence 6

Go On

Going Up?

She could walk up three flights of stairs or the elevator. Lola joined the
  (1)   (2)
group waiting for the elevator. Then a voice inside her began to speak.
                                       (3)
"Get going, your body needs the exercise!" it said. Halfway up the
  (4)   (5)
stairs, Lola heard the elevator bell ringing. The elevator had gotten
                                          (6)
stuck between floors. Now its passengers would have to wait inside
                              (7)
until it could be repaired.

---

5. Which sentence would best begin this paragraph?

- (A) Many people worked in the building.
- (B) Lola had a choice to make.
- (C) Most city buildings have several floors.
- (D) Elevators have alarm bells.

6. How is sentence 1 best written?

- (A) She could walk the stairs or the elevator.
- (B) Walk up three flights of stairs, she could, or the elevator.
- (C) She could walk up three flights of stairs or take the elevator.
- (D) Walk up the stairs or the elevator is what she could do.

7. Which word is best to use in place of *speak* in sentence 3?

- (A) report
- (B) talk
- (C) sing
- (D) nag

8. The author probably wrote this passage to –

- (A) describe an alarm sound
- (B) tell an interesting story
- (C) explain how elevators work
- (D) give advice about exercise

Go On

You Don't Say

In the early years of our country, men and women followed strict
(1)
rules for talking with one another. One rule was that words for parts of
(2)
the body should not be used. Other words that were more polite were
(3)
to be used in place of words for body parts. Today people think this
(4)
rule is silly. An Englishman who visited the United States got a lesson
(5)
in politeness. When he saw a woman fall down, he asked if she had
(6)
hurt her leg. His question upset the woman a great deal. She told him
(7)   (8)
that a man should not use the word *leg* when speaking to a woman.

Instead he should have asked her if she had hurt her limb.
(9)

---

9. Where would you be most likely to read this passage?

Ⓐ in a newspaper

Ⓑ in a book about England

Ⓒ in a letter

Ⓓ in a book about American history

10. Which sentence does **not** belong in this passage?

Ⓐ sentence 1

Ⓑ sentence 4

Ⓒ sentence 6

Ⓓ sentence 9

11. How is sentence 3 best written?

Ⓐ Other words that were more polite were to be used instead.

Ⓑ Words that were more polite were to be used in place of the words that were not polite.

Ⓒ Other words that were polite were to be used in place of words that were not polite.

Ⓓ Instead of words that were not polite, words that were polite were to be used.

12. Which word is best used in place of *got* in sentence 5?

Ⓐ gained

Ⓑ had

Ⓒ received

Ⓓ learned

Go On →

A Good Cook's Secrets

Planning and patience are the secrets to being a good cook.
(1)
Planning involves having all the ingredients you will need for a dish
(2)
before you start cooking. Patience means getting the batter smooth
(3)
enough or the sauce thick enough for a dish to come out right.

Planning also involves giving yourself enough time to follow each step
(4)
of a recipe. A good carpenter also knows the importance of planning
(5)
and patience. With planning and patience, even a beginner can cook a
(6)
great meal.

13. Which sentence could be added after sentence 1?

Ⓐ There are many good cookbooks.

Ⓑ Every great chef knows these two secrets.

Ⓒ Buy the best cooking tools.

Ⓓ Cooking lessons are fun and helpful.

14. Which sentence does **not** belong in this passage?

Ⓐ sentence 2

Ⓑ sentence 3

Ⓒ sentence 4

Ⓓ sentence 5

15. How can the order of the sentences in this passage be improved?

Ⓐ Move sentence 3 to the beginning.

Ⓑ Move sentence 4 right after sentence 2.

Ⓒ Move sentence 4 to the end.

Ⓓ Move sentence 6 right after sentence 3.

16. What is the topic sentence of this passage?

Ⓐ sentence 1

Ⓑ sentence 2

Ⓒ sentence 3

Ⓓ sentence 4

Stop

Mathematics

PRACTICE 24 • Interpreting Data

SAMPLES

Directions: Reggie made this tally chart showing how many times he did each chore during the week. Use the chart to answer the questions.

Kind of Chore	Number of Times Done
Making bed	卌 II
Feeding dog	卌 卌 IIII
Washing dishes	卌 IIII
Dusting	II
Folding laundry	IIII
Setting table	卌 卌 I

A. How many times did Reggie fold laundry?

Ⓐ 11 Ⓒ 4
Ⓑ 5 Ⓓ 2

B. Which chore did Reggie do most?

Ⓐ Making bed
Ⓑ Feeding dog
Ⓒ Washing dishes
Ⓓ Setting table

Tips and Reminders
- Study the chart or graph carefully. Use it to answer the questions.
- After choosing an answer, read the question again to make sure you have answered it correctly.

PRACTICE

Directions: This chart shows the shipping charges for a mail-order company. Use the chart to answer questions 1–2.

Cost of Order	Shipping Charge
less than $25.00	$5.75
$25.00– $49.99	$6.95
$50.00– $100.00	$8.50
more than $100.00	$9.75

1. Gloria ordered a coat that cost $81.99. What is the shipping charge for her order?

Ⓐ $5.75 Ⓒ $8.50
Ⓑ $6.95 Ⓓ $9.75

2. What is the shipping charge for an order that costs $11.50?

Ⓐ $5.75 Ⓒ $8.50
Ⓑ $6.95 Ⓓ $9.75

Go On

Directions: A juice company asked people to try out its new juice flavors. This bar graph shows what people liked. Use the graph to answer questions 3–5.

Favorite Juice Flavors

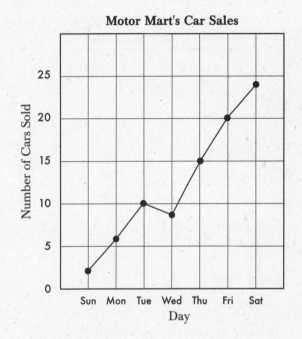

Directions: This graph shows the number of cars bought at Motor Mart in one week. Use the graph to answer questions 6–8.

3. Which juice flavor was most popular?

Ⓐ Apple   Ⓒ Grape

Ⓑ Cherry   Ⓓ Strawberry

4. How many people liked Apple best?

Ⓐ 20   Ⓒ 35

Ⓑ 25   Ⓓ 40

5. How many more people chose Cherry than Grape as their favorite flavor?

Ⓐ 10   Ⓒ 40

Ⓑ 20   Ⓓ 60

6. How many cars were sold on Thursday?

Ⓐ 6   Ⓒ 8

Ⓑ 10   Ⓓ 15

7. On which day were the fewest cars sold?

Ⓐ Sunday   Ⓒ Tuesday

Ⓑ Monday   Ⓓ Saturday

8. How many more cars were sold on Friday than on Tuesday?

Ⓐ 5   Ⓒ 15

Ⓑ 10   Ⓓ 20

Go On

Directions: This graph shows how many people from four different towns ran in the Bay County Road Race. Use the graph to answer questions 9–11.

Bay County Road Race

Littleton	🏃🏃🏃🏃🏃
Seabury	🏃🏃🏃🏃🏃🏃🏃
Arkville	🏃🏃🏃🏃🏃🏃🏃🏃🏃
Mansfield	🏃🏃🏃

🏃 = 5 runners

9. The fewest runners came from –

Ⓐ Littleton   Ⓒ Arkville

Ⓑ Seabury   Ⓓ Mansfield

10. How many more runners were there from Seabury than from Mansfield?

Ⓐ 35   Ⓒ 15

Ⓑ 20   Ⓓ 5

11. How many runners were there from these four towns altogether?

Ⓐ 260   Ⓒ 52

Ⓑ 130   Ⓓ 26

Directions: This chart shows regular and sale prices of clothing at Kids' World. Use the chart to answer questions 12–14.

Kids' World Clothing Prices

Clothing	Regular Price	Sale Price
Sweatshirt	$10.99	$8.99
Sweatpants	$12.00	$11.00
T-shirt	$7.50	$5.00
Jeans	$25.00	$20.00

12. How much does a T-shirt cost at the regular price?

Ⓐ $12.00   Ⓒ $7.50

Ⓑ $10.00   Ⓓ $5.00

13. How much could you save by buying a pair of jeans on sale?

Ⓐ $5.00   Ⓒ $2.00

Ⓑ $2.50   Ⓓ $1.00

14. How much would you spend if you bought sweatpants and a sweatshirt on sale?

Ⓐ $19.99   Ⓒ $21.99

Ⓑ $20.99   Ⓓ $22.99

Go On

Directions: This table shows how many students do after-school activities. Use the table to answer questions 15–17.

Number of Students Per Grade in After-School Activities

Activity	Grade 5	Grade 6	Grade 7	Grade 8
Sports	18	21	13	15
Band	9	14	8	20
Newspaper	3	7	5	6
Art Club	9	12	16	4

15. Which activity has the fewest students altogether?

  Ⓐ Sports   Ⓒ Newspaper

  Ⓑ Band   Ⓓ Art Club

16. In Art Club, the largest number of students come from –

  Ⓐ Grade 5   Ⓒ Grade 7

  Ⓑ Grade 6   Ⓓ Grade 8

17. How many students in Grade 8 take part in Band?

  Ⓐ 45   Ⓒ 15

  Ⓑ 20   Ⓓ 14

Directions: This chart shows how many different states' license plates Doug counted on a bus trip. Use the chart to answer questions 18–20.

State	Number of License Plates Seen
Indiana	┼┼┼ ┼┼┼ III
Michigan	┼┼┼ ┼┼┼ ┼┼┼ IIII
New York	┼┼┼ II
Ohio	┼┼┼ ┼┼┼ I
Pennsylvania	┼┼┼ II
West Virginia	IIII

18. Which state's license plate did Doug see most often?

  Ⓐ Indiana

  Ⓑ Michigan

  Ⓒ Ohio

  Ⓓ Pennsylvania

19. How many license plates did Doug see from New York?

  Ⓐ 12   Ⓒ 7

  Ⓑ 11   Ⓓ 4

20. How many more license plates from Indiana did Doug see than plates from West Virginia?

  Ⓐ 3   Ⓒ 9

  Ⓑ 7   Ⓓ 15

Reading

PRACTICE 25 • Evaluating Information

Directions: Read each passage. Then answer the questions that follow.

SAMPLES

Dear Editor:
  The corner of Ballantine and Second is a very dangerous intersection. Second Street has stop signs, but Ballantine does not. Drivers on Second often think that it is a four-way stop, so they pull out in front of oncoming traffic! Just last week a man was driving his station wagon down Ballantine, and a big blue van pulled right out in front of him. It was obvious that the other driver thought the station wagon had to stop.
  I have written three letters to the city, but nothing has been done. The city obviously doesn't care about its citizens. I am hoping that the newspaper can put a little pressure on the city to improve this intersection.

Hunter Atwater

A. Which sentence states an opinion?

Ⓐ Second Street has stop signs, but Ballantine does not.

Ⓑ I have written three letters to the city, but nothing has been done.

Ⓒ The city obviously doesn't care about its citizens.

Ⓓ Just last week a man was driving down Ballantine.

B. The author's description of the station wagon's near-accident supports the idea that

Ⓐ most people are not good drivers

Ⓑ drivers of vans are dangerous

Ⓒ the city doesn't care about its citizens

Ⓓ the intersection of Ballantine and Second is dangerous

Tips and Reminders

• A fact is a statement that can be proven true. An opinion is a statement, belief, or feeling that cannot be proven true.

• To find evidence to support an idea, look for details in the passage that are connected to the idea.

Go On →

PRACTICE

Directions: Read this passage about computers. Then answer questions 1–4.

> How many times have you heard people say that computers don't make mistakes? Well, they are wrong.
>
> Last week I found a rather large mistake on my telephone bill. The computer charged me 4 million dollars for a 2-minute call to China! Wow, I told the phone company, that's a large bill for a phone call I did not even make. The phone company person told me that the bill must be correct because it was calculated by a computer. That was the least intelligent response I have ever heard.
>
> Recently, I read about a young couple in Arizona. One night a squad of armed police officers broke into their house and arrested them. As it turns out, the police had the wrong house. A computer printed the wrong address on a report, and the police believed the computer.
>
> Computers don't make mistakes? I disagree. Computers are only as accurate as the people who operate them.

1. Which sentence states an opinion?

   Ⓐ The computer charged me 4 million dollars.

   Ⓑ That was the least intelligent response I have ever heard.

   Ⓒ Recently, I read about a young couple in Arizona.

   Ⓓ A computer printed the wrong address on a report.

2. In which source would you most likely find articles about other computer errors?

   Ⓐ encyclopedia

   Ⓑ dictionary

   Ⓒ social studies textbook

   Ⓓ newspaper

3. Which sentence states a fact?

   Ⓐ Wow, that's a large bill.

   Ⓑ That was the least intelligent response I have ever heard.

   Ⓒ A computer printed the wrong address on a report.

   Ⓓ Computers are only as accurate as the people who operate them.

4. Which detail supports the idea that computers make mistakes?

   Ⓐ Police in Arizona arrested the wrong people.

   Ⓑ The phone company person said that the bill must be correct.

   Ⓒ Phone bills are printed by computers.

   Ⓓ People say that computers don't make mistakes.

Go On

Directions: Read this passage about putting together a birdhouse. Then answer questions 5–7.

How to Assemble Your Birdhouse

Congratulations! You have just bought the finest birdhouse available today. With proper assembly and care, this birdhouse will give years of safe shelter to your favorite feathered friends.

To put together this birdhouse, first make sure you have all the pieces (see the parts list). Find the floor piece. Attach the back and side wall pieces to the floor with the nails. Do not paint the inside walls. The smell of paint or wood stain discourages birds from nesting inside. Next, add the front wall and roof. Young birds use the notches on the inside of the front wall to climb up to the entry hole.

The dowel serves as the entry perch. Coat one end of the dowel with wood glue and put it into the small hole under the entry hole on the front wall. Let it dry.

Hang the birdhouse in a safe place out of reach of cats and other hunters. Make sure you can see it from a convenient window.

Enjoy the house and your new feathered neighbors!

---

5. Which sentence states an opinion?

(A) You have just bought the finest birdhouse available today.

(B) Attach the back and side wall pieces to the floor with the nails.

(C) The smell of paint or wood stain discourages birds from nesting inside.

(D) Young birds use the notches on the inside of the front wall to climb up to the entry hole.

6. If you wanted to find more information about the nesting habits of birds, which would probably be the best source?

(A) dictionary

(B) *A Handbook for Woodworking*

(C) newspaper

(D) *A Field Guide to Birds*

7. Which detail supports the idea that you should not paint the birdhouse?

(A) Plain wood lasts longer than painted wood.

(B) Birds don't like the smell of paint.

(C) Wood stain looks better than paint.

(D) Baby birds might eat the paint.

Go On →

Directions: Read this passage about the Inuit way of life. Then answer questions 8–10.

For thousands of years, the Inuit and their predecessors built houses of snow to keep themselves warm and safe in the long, cold Arctic winter. It took a skilled eye and a lot of experience to build a snow house. But a good builder could make a snow house in just a few hours, and it had room for a whole family.

To make a snow house, the builder would cut blocks of hard-packed snow. He would then stack the blocks on top of one another in a circular shape. While the builder carefully cut and placed the blocks, other members of the family packed loose snow into the cracks between the blocks. A small hole would be left at the very top to let out smoke. Then the builder would cut a small opening for a door and build a low tunnel extending outward from it.

Once it was built, a snow house was fairly comfortable. An oil lamp was used for cooking and heating, and the indoor temperature just a foot off the floor could reach 50 degrees Fahrenheit. These snow houses were used primarily to house family members while they traveled, and the house would be abandoned after a day or two when it was time to move on. But for temporary shelter, the snow house was a fairly pleasant home in the middle of the harsh Arctic climate.

8. Which sentence states an opinion?

   (A) A snow house had room for a whole family.

   (B) The builder would cut blocks of hard-packed snow.

   (C) A small hole would be left at the very top to let out smoke.

   (D) But for temporary shelter, the snow house was a fairly pleasant home.

9. Which would be a good source of information about average temperatures in the Arctic at various times of the year?

   (A) a newspaper

   (B) an almanac

   (C) a social studies textbook

   (D) an on-line catalog

10. Which detail supports the idea that a snow house was fairly comfortable?

   (A) It took a skilled eye and a lot of experience to build a snow house.

   (B) The indoor temperature just a foot off the floor could reach 50 degrees Fahrenheit.

   (C) These snow houses were used primarily to house family members while they traveled.

   (D) The house would be abandoned after a day or two.

Stop

PRACTICE 26 • Study Skills

Directions: Choose the best answer to each question about finding information.

SAMPLES

A. Which word would come first in alphabetical order?

- Ⓐ ledge
- Ⓒ length
- Ⓑ left
- Ⓓ lecture

B. In which part of the library would you find a book about the life of W.E.B. Dubois?

- Ⓐ the fiction section
- Ⓑ the biography section
- Ⓒ the sports section
- Ⓓ the reference section

C. Which is a main index heading that includes the other three words?

- Ⓐ Crocodile
- Ⓒ Snake
- Ⓑ Reptile
- Ⓓ Alligator

D. To find a map of your state, you should look in –

- Ⓐ an encyclopedia
- Ⓑ a telephone directory
- Ⓒ an atlas
- Ⓓ a dictionary

Tips and Reminders

- To put words in alphabetical order, look at the first letter of each word, then the second, third, and so on.
- To find an index heading, look for a main topic that describes the other three choices.
- Use key words in the question to figure out what kind of information is needed.

PRACTICE

1. Which city would be listed first in alphabetical order?

- Ⓐ Tangiers
- Ⓒ Tampa
- Ⓑ Tallahassee
- Ⓓ Tara

2. Which word would be listed first in a glossary?

- Ⓐ calendar
- Ⓒ calibrate
- Ⓑ calculator
- Ⓓ calligraphy

Go On

3. Which is a main index heading that includes the other three words?

Ⓐ Japan

Ⓑ Spain

Ⓒ France

Ⓓ Country

4. Which is a main index heading that includes the other three words?

Ⓐ Saturn

Ⓑ Planet

Ⓒ Jupiter

Ⓓ Mars

5. In which section of the library would you find a biographical dictionary?

Ⓐ the reference section

Ⓑ the fiction section

Ⓒ the travel section

Ⓓ the nonfiction section

6. In which part of a science textbook should you look up the meaning of the word *asteroid?*

Ⓐ title page

Ⓑ table of contents

Ⓒ index

Ⓓ glossary

Directions: Brett is making an outline for a report on seashells. Use the outline to answer questions 7–8.

Seashells

I. _____
   A. Bivalve
   B. Spiral
   C. Other shapes

II. Collecting shells
   A. Gather shells
   B. Clean and oil shells
   C. _____

7. Which topic best fits in the blank beside I?

Ⓐ Why I Like Shells

Ⓑ Colors of Shells

Ⓒ Living in the Sea

Ⓓ Kinds of Shells

8. Which subtopic best fits in the blank beside II.C?

Ⓐ Display shells

Ⓑ How to collect them

Ⓒ Finding a beach

Ⓓ Digging in the sand

Go On →

Directions: Deeksha is writing a report about India, the country where she was born. Choose the best answer to each question about finding information for her report.

9. To find information about religions in India, Deeksha should look in –

   (A) a dictionary

   (B) a newspaper

   (C) an atlas

   (D) an encyclopedia

10. In what source would Deeksha most likely find information about recent elections in India?

    (A) dictionary

    (B) news magazine

    (C) atlas

    (D) encyclopedia

11. To find out where the Ganges River is located, Deeksha should look in –

    (A) an atlas

    (B) a newspaper

    (C) a science textbook

    (D) a dictionary

12. In what part of a social studies textbook should she look to find the meaning of the word *textiles?*

    (A) table of contents

    (B) title page

    (C) index

    (D) glossary

Directions: Use this part of an index from a book about India to answer questions 13–15.

Brahmins. *See* Caste system.
Caste system, 83–85
Economy, 123–143
　　agricultural products, 123–128
　　industries, 129–134
　　trade, 139–142
Gandhi, Indira, 72–73
Gandhi, Mahatma, 64–65, 71
Geography, 12–24
Government, 101–105

13. On which pages would you find information about the role of farming in India's economy?

    (A) pages 83–85

    (B) pages 123–128

    (C) pages 129–134

    (D) pages 139–142

14. For information about the Brahmins, you should look under –

    (A) Geography

    (B) Government

    (C) History

    (D) Caste system

15. On which pages would you find information about Indira Gandhi?

    (A) pages 12–24

    (B) pages 64–65

    (C) pages 72–73

    (D) pages 101–105

Go On

Julia is preparing to write a report on Guatemala. Use the title page and table of contents from a book about Guatemala to answer questions 16–20.

The People's Artists:
Contemporary Guatemalan Folk Artists

by Sam Joyabaj
photographs by Santiago Sololá

La Familia Press
Mexico City

Contents

1. The Mayan Tradition   1
2. Painters   23
3. Sculptors   47
4. Weavers   71
5. Wood Carvers   96
6. Potters   117
7. The Future   125

16. Who wrote this book?

 (A) Contemporary Guatemalans
 (B) Sam Joyabaj
 (C) Santiago Sololá
 (D) La Familia

17. This book is mainly about –

 (A) Sam Joyabaj
 (B) the population of Guatemala
 (C) folk artists
 (D) the history of Guatemala

18. Which chapter contains information about pottery in Guatemala?

 (A) Chapter 3
 (B) Chapter 4
 (C) Chapter 5
 (D) Chapter 6

19. On which page should Julia begin reading about people who make carpets and wall hangings?

 (A) page 23
 (B) page 47
 (C) page 71
 (D) page 96

20. This book was published by –

 (A) La Familia Press
 (B) The Mayan Tradition
 (C) Mexico City
 (D) Santiago Sololá

Stop

Mathematics

PRACTICE 27 • Solving Problems

Directions: Choose the best answer to each problem.

SAMPLES

A. Eleven students in the garden club want to grow bonsai trees. The trees cost $12.00 each. Which number sentence should be used to find how much money is needed to buy one tree for each student?

Ⓐ $11 \times \$12.00 = \square$

Ⓑ $11 + \$12.00 = \square$

Ⓒ $11 - \$12.00 = \square$

Ⓓ $11 \div \$12.00 = \square$

B. Alan earns $15 each week taking care of his neighbor's plants. What additional information do you need to figure out how long it will take him to earn enough money to buy a guitar?

Ⓐ how many hours he works

Ⓑ how much the guitar costs

Ⓒ how long Alan has had the job

Ⓓ how many plants he cares for

Tips and Reminders

- Underline or jot down important information to help you answer each question.

- Check each answer choice.

- Draw a picture if it helps you answer the question.

- When a question asks <u>about</u> how many or how much, use rounding to estimate your answer.

PRACTICE

1. A box of crackers costs $1.79. Which number sentence could be used to find the cost of 5 boxes of crackers?

Ⓐ $\$1.79 \div 5 = \square$

Ⓑ $\square \times 5 = \$1.79$

Ⓒ $\$1.79 \times 5 = \square$

Ⓓ $\$1.79 + 5 = \square$

2. Brian has 32 pages of stamps in a binder. Each page holds about 20 stamps. <u>About</u> how many stamps does he have in all?

Ⓐ 800   Ⓒ 80

Ⓑ 600   Ⓓ 60

Go On

3. Spencer worked from 3:00 P.M. to 5:00 P.M. on Monday. On Wednesday, he started work at 4:00 P.M. He worked for 3 hours on Friday. What other information do you need to find how many hours he worked in all?

Ⓐ what kind of work he did

Ⓑ when he finished on Wednesday

Ⓒ what time he started on Friday

Ⓓ how much he earned

4. The art classes at a school use nine 48-lb bags of clay each week. <u>About</u> how much clay do they use in all each week?

Ⓐ 300 lb   Ⓒ 400 lb

Ⓑ 360 lb   Ⓓ 450 lb

5. Samantha spent a total of $22.00 to make 6 treat bags for a birthday party. Which number sentence could be used to find how much each bag cost?

Ⓐ $6 \times \$22.00 = \square$

Ⓑ $\$22.00 \div 6 = \square$

Ⓒ $6 + \$22.00 = \square$

Ⓓ $\$22.00 - 6 = \square$

6. There are 3 tennis balls in each can and 36 cans in a box. Which question could you answer with this information?

Ⓐ How many tennis balls are in a box?

Ⓑ What is the cost of 1 can?

Ⓒ How many balls will be used?

Ⓓ What is the cost of 1 box?

7. If you throw out 3.5 pounds of garbage each day, <u>about</u> how much do you throw out each month?

Ⓐ between 60 and 80 lb

Ⓑ between 80 and 100 lb

Ⓒ between 100 and 120 lb

Ⓓ between 120 and 140 lb

8. By the end of 1993, a total of 308 people had traveled into space and 113 were from countries other than the United States. Which sentence could be used to find how many Americans traveled in space?

Ⓐ $308 \times 113 = \square$

Ⓑ $308 - 113 = \square$

Ⓒ $308 \div 113 = \square$

Ⓓ $308 + 113 = \square$

9. Sarah wants to buy 3 geraniums and 3 petunias. The geraniums cost $1.99 each. What information do you need to find out if $10.00 is enough to buy the 6 plants?

Ⓐ the colors of the flowers

Ⓑ the cost of petunias

Ⓒ how many plants she has at home

Ⓓ how much change she will get

10. Ron bought 2 books for $7.95 each. The sales tax was $0.90. Which number sentence could be used to find how much Ron spent in all?

Ⓐ $(2 \times \$7.95) + \$0.90 = \square$

Ⓑ $2 + \$7.95 + \$0.90 = \square$

Ⓒ $(2 \times \$0.90) + \$7.95 = \square$

Ⓓ $(2 \times \$7.95) - \$0.90 = \square$

Go On

11. Liza needs 3.15 gallons of paint for one room, 2.95 gallons for a second room, and 4.05 gallons for a third room. <u>About</u> how many gallons of paint does she need in all?

Ⓐ 5 gallons

Ⓑ 10 gallons

Ⓒ 15 gallons

Ⓓ 20 gallons

12. Six children want to share a box of crackers evenly. There are 33 crackers in the box. Which sentence could be used to find out how many crackers each child gets?

Ⓐ $33 \times 6 = \square$

Ⓑ $33 - \square = 6$

Ⓒ $33 \div 6 = \square$

Ⓓ $33 + \square = 6$

13. Fifteen baseball players gave $2.00 each to get a present for their coach. Three parents gave $5.00 each. Which sentence could be used to find how much money the team had in all?

Ⓐ $(15 \times \$2.00) + (3 \times \$5.00) = \square$

Ⓑ $(15 \times \$2.00) + \$5.00 = \square$

Ⓒ $(15 \times \$2.00 \times \$5.00) = \square$

Ⓓ $15 \times (\$2.00 + \$5.00) = \square$

14. A box of beans weighs $\frac{3}{4}$ lb. Which sentence could be used to find how much 5 boxes weigh?

Ⓐ $5 \times \frac{3}{4} = \square$

Ⓑ $5 - \frac{3}{4} = \square$

Ⓒ $5 \div \frac{3}{4} = \square$

Ⓓ $5 + \frac{3}{4} = \square$

15. Students at a school held 3 car washes. They made $179.35 at the first, $305.05 at the second, and $195.50 at the third. <u>About</u> how much did they raise in all?

Ⓐ between $550 and $600

Ⓑ between $600 and $650

Ⓒ between $650 and $700

Ⓓ between $700 and $750

16. Eli was 4 days late when he returned his books to the library. He had to pay a fine of $0.25 per book for each day it was late. What other information do you need to figure out how much Eli had to pay the library for his late fines?

Ⓐ how many books he returned late

Ⓑ when he borrowed the books

Ⓒ which books he borrowed

Ⓓ when he returned the books

Stop

Reading

PRACTICE 28 •. Making Judgments

Directions: Read each passage. Then answer the questions that follow.

SAMPLES

Fellow citizens of Springfield, I am grateful for your support in this election, and I promise to do my best to serve this city. Before this term is over, I will have five more police officers walking our streets. I will break ground for a new grade school. I will push for changes in our zoning laws. And with the building of the new Springfield Community Kitchen, I will make sure that no one in this town goes hungry!

With your support, I will do everything in my power to make Springfield the best place to live in all of America!

Thank you once again.

A. The author's main purpose in this speech is to –

Ⓐ remind voters of her promises

Ⓑ tell people about the Community Kitchen

Ⓒ describe new goals for the city

Ⓓ thank the voters for their support

B. Which of the speaker's promises will be most difficult to keep?

Ⓐ hiring more police officers

Ⓑ making Springfield the best place to live in America

Ⓒ building a new school

Ⓓ opening a community kitchen

Tips and Reminders

• As you read a passage, think about what the author is trying to say or why the author wrote the passage.

• To make a judgment or decision, think about the information in the passage. Look at all the answer choices and choose the most likely or most important one.

Go On →

PRACTICE

> *From pure nature comes Pure Springs water . . .*
>
> Pure Springs water starts high in the mountains where glaciers melt slowly, making tiny streams of icy cold, clear water. These streams filter their way down the mountains, joining others to form small, crystal rivers.
>
> And that's where Pure Springs water comes from. It's never processed. It's never stored in tanks. And it's never mixed with chemicals. It's just bottled right away in our ultra-modern plant and shipped to a store near you.
>
> These days, tap water contains a lot more than just water. It leaches metals out of the pipes. It picks up algae. And it contains chlorine to keep things from growing in it.
>
> But Pure Springs is different. It's bottled so quickly and at such cold temperatures that no treatments are needed. So all you get is pure, natural, healthful water.
>
> So give Pure Springs a try. You'll never go back to the tap.

1. The author's main purpose in writing this passage is to –

   Ⓐ give information about spring water

   Ⓑ explain how rivers are formed

   Ⓒ describe the advantages of cold water

   Ⓓ persuade people to buy Pure Springs water

2. Which of the author's statements would be hardest to prove?

   Ⓐ You'll never drink tap water again.

   Ⓑ Streams flow into rivers.

   Ⓒ Tap water contains chlorine.

   Ⓓ Pure Springs water is never stored in tanks.

3. The author seems to think that the best drinking water is –

   Ⓐ treated with chemicals

   Ⓑ naturally pure

   Ⓒ tasteless

   Ⓓ colorful

4. The author of this passage wants readers to believe that Pure Springs water –

   Ⓐ will make you happy

   Ⓑ is best when it is warm

   Ⓒ is better than tap water

   Ⓓ is a good value for the cost

Go On →

To the Promotions Department:

As president of Apex Novelties, I must say I am pleased with the surprising events that you have staged lately. As you know, we are the area's largest maker of unusual costumes. Yet too many people haven't heard of us. You are doing a great job of fixing that problem.

One of my favorite stunts was when the coach of the basketball team wore our Charlie Chaplin costume during the opening game of the season. I guess that more than 25,000 people saw the costume and our corporate logo on his back. Nice work!

And how did you get Susan Ziegler to do her weather forecast while wearing our Dolphin costume? She looked positively silly, and everyone in town was talking about it the next day.

But the best thing was when you got the mayor to hold a City Council meeting while wearing our Tiny Ballerina costume! He looked outrageous, and his picture made the front page of the *Herald-Telegram!*

Please keep up the good work. If our promotions continue on this track, I'll see to it that you get a double bonus at the end of the year.

Malcolm Richter
President, Apex Novelties

5. Mr. Richter cares if people are seen in Apex costumes because –

 Ⓐ they look silly

 Ⓑ he wants people to laugh

 Ⓒ he thinks it will increase sales

 Ⓓ he likes to wear them too

6. Mr. Richter hopes that people will –

 Ⓐ vote against the mayor

 Ⓑ laugh about the costumes

 Ⓒ buy more Apex costumes

 Ⓓ expect to see costumes every day

7. What pleases Mr. Richter most about the members of the Promotions Department?

 Ⓐ They wear costumes to work.

 Ⓑ They make sure a lot of people see Apex costumes.

 Ⓒ They support the mayor.

 Ⓓ They use unpaid models.

8. Mr. Richter's main purpose in this letter is to –

 Ⓐ thank the Promotions Department

 Ⓑ complain about low sales

 Ⓒ give information about Apex

 Ⓓ describe some silly events

Go On

The tunnel to the cave was smaller than Diane had expected. It was just barely big enough for her to squeeze through.

"You're doing fine, Diane," said Mrs. Columbo from behind her.

Diane felt the walls of the tunnel pressing against her, and she swallowed hard. She squirmed ahead until the passage opened into a small chamber. Several other students were already there.

"Now, class," Mrs. Columbo said, "let's see how much light there is down here. Everyone turn off your flashlights."

The lights clicked off. Instantly, the room became completely dark. Not just dark like a dark night or a bedroom just after the lights go off. Here in the cave, there was no light at all. Diane put her hand right in front of her face, but she couldn't see a thing.

At first, the darkness felt scary. But as she gradually adjusted to the darkness, Diane began to feel a sense of security. No one could see her. It was as though she was invisible.

When the flashlights came back on, everyone turned to head back out of the cave. But it was different now. Something had changed. The passage that had seemed so small and cramped before now felt like a cozy den. Diane had no trouble wriggling back out.

9. The author's main purpose in this passage is to –

Ⓐ tell an entertaining story

Ⓑ give information about caves

Ⓒ persuade people to explore caves

Ⓓ describe Mrs. Columbo

10. At the beginning of the story, what was Diane most afraid of?

Ⓐ having someone see her

Ⓑ losing her flashlight

Ⓒ making too much noise

Ⓓ being in a small, enclosed place

11. Based on evidence in the story, the teacher most likely took her class into the cave to –

Ⓐ make them feel afraid

Ⓑ have fun on a hot afternoon

Ⓒ test the fitness of her students

Ⓓ learn about caves

12. The author of this story probably feels that caves are –

Ⓐ dangerous

Ⓑ terrifying

Ⓒ fascinating

Ⓓ boring

Stop

Language Arts

PRACTICE 29 • Reference Materials

SAMPLES

Directions: Choose the best answer to each question.

A. Which guide words could be found on the same dictionary page as the word *pagoda?*

Ⓐ pamper/panda

Ⓑ padlock/pale

Ⓒ panorama/paperback

Ⓓ pace/paddy

B. If you wanted to look in an encyclopedia for information about the machines invented by Thomas Edison, you should look under –

Ⓐ machines

Ⓑ inventions

Ⓒ Thomas

Ⓓ Edison

Tips and Reminders

• In a dictionary, guide words show the first and last entries on a dictionary page.

• Look for key words to help answer each question.

• Study the chart, map, or diagram carefully. Use it to find the answer to each question.

PRACTICE

1. Which guide words could be found on the same dictionary page as the word *graffiti?*

Ⓐ gourd/grackle

Ⓑ gram/granddad

Ⓒ grade/grain

Ⓓ grasp/grave

2. Which guide words could be found on the same dictionary page as the word *rebel?*

Ⓐ reason/rebus

Ⓑ recess/recognize

Ⓒ read/reap

Ⓓ razor/react

Go On

Directions: Use this part of a dictionary page to answer questions 3–7.

---

magnesium • mall

mag•ne•si•um (mag nē' zē əm) *n.*, A common, silver-white metallic element found in nature. It is often used in fireworks because it burns with a bright white light.
mag•net (**mag'** nət) *n.*, *pl.* **magnets**. A piece of metal, stone, or other material that attracts iron.
mag•net•ic (mag net' ik) *adj.*, **1.** Acting like a magnet; of or relating to magnets or magnetism. **2.** Able to attract people.
mag•nif•i•cent (mag **nif'** ə sənt) *adj.*, Grand and very beautiful.
mag•no•lia (mag **nōl'** yə) *n.*, *pl.*, **magnolias**. A shrub or tree with large white, yellow, rose, or purple blossoms.
mag•pie (**mag'** pī) *n.*, *pl.*, **magpies**. A noisy bird with long tail and thick bill.
ma•hog•a•ny (mə **hog'** ə nē) *n.*, *pl.*, **mahoganies**. **1.** An evergreen tree that yields a strong, hard, reddish brown wood. **2.** A reddish brown color. *adj.* Having a reddish brown color.

Pronunciation Guide

a pat	o pot	ə represents:
ā pay	ō go	a in **ago**
ä father	ô for	e in **item**
e pet	o͝o book	i in **pencil**
ē be	o͞o boot	o in **atom**
i pit	u cut	u in **circus**
ī pie	û fur	

3. What does *magnificent* mean?

Ⓐ reddish brown

Ⓑ acting like a magnet

Ⓒ grand and very beautiful

Ⓓ having white or yellow blossoms

4. What is *magnesium?*

Ⓐ a kind of metal

Ⓑ a shrub or tree

Ⓒ a noisy bird

Ⓓ a stone that attracts iron

5. Which is the correct way to divide the word *mahogany* into syllables?

Ⓐ m-ah-og-any

Ⓑ ma-ho-ga-ny

Ⓒ ma-hog-an-y

Ⓓ ma-hog-a-ny

6. The *o* in *magnolia* is pronounced like the *o* in –

Ⓐ pot

Ⓑ go

Ⓒ for

Ⓓ book

7. Which word best describes someone who attracts other people?

Ⓐ mahogany

Ⓑ magpie

Ⓒ magnetic

Ⓓ magnolia

Go On

PRACTICE 29 • Reference Materials (continued)

Directions: Use the encyclopedia volumes to answer questions 8–10.

8. Which volume would tell you most about the tools made in Europe and Asia during the Iron Age?

Ⓐ Volume 3   Ⓒ Volume 9

Ⓑ Volume 4   Ⓓ Volume 10

9. Which volume would tell you most about the "fireside chats" that President Franklin D. Roosevelt conducted on the radio?

Ⓐ Volume 2   Ⓒ Volume 7

Ⓑ Volume 3   Ⓓ Volume 8

10. In which volume should you look for information about how coal is formed, mined, and used?

Ⓐ Volume 2   Ⓒ Volume 5

Ⓑ Volume 3   Ⓓ Volume 10

Directions: Use this library catalog card to answer questions 11–13.

> INVENTORS–WORLD
>
> 920 Edwards, Franco
> Ed   From da Vinci to Edison / by
>   Franco Edwards; illustrated by Susan Martin.
>   –Greenville: Doubletime, 1998.
>   114 p. : ill.; 23 cm.
>
>   1. Inventors–World–Biography. 2.
>   Inventors–World–History.
>   I. Edwards, Franco. II. Title: From da Vinci to Edison.

11. What kind of catalog entry is this?

Ⓐ a title listing

Ⓑ a subject listing

Ⓒ an author listing

Ⓓ a publisher listing

12. What is the title of this book?

Ⓐ From da Vinci to Edison

Ⓑ Franco Edwards

Ⓒ Susan Martin

Ⓓ Doubletime

13. What is the call number for this book?

Ⓐ 114 p.   Ⓒ 23 cm

Ⓑ 1998   Ⓓ 920 Ed

Go On →

Directions: The map below shows the central part of a town and some of its important buildings. Use the map to answer questions 14–18.

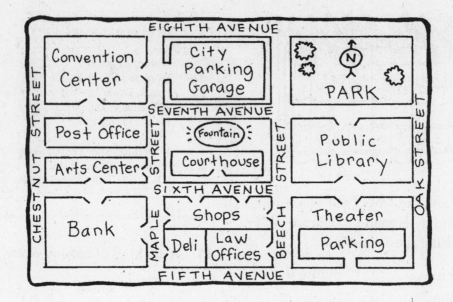

14. From which street can you enter the parking garage?

   Ⓐ Oak Street
   Ⓑ Beech Street
   Ⓒ Maple Street
   Ⓓ Chestnut Street

15. Which of these is closest to the Convention Center?

   Ⓐ Theater   Ⓒ Law Offices
   Ⓑ Post Office   Ⓓ Park

16. In what direction must you go to walk from the Bank to the Convention Center?

   Ⓐ north   Ⓒ east
   Ⓑ south   Ⓓ west

17. The Theater is in a block formed by Fifth Avenue and –

   Ⓐ Chestnut Street
   Ⓑ Maple Street
   Ⓒ Eighth Avenue
   Ⓓ Sixth Avenue

18. Which is the shortest route from the Deli to the Public Library?

   Ⓐ Go west on Fifth Avenue and north on Chestnut Street.
   Ⓑ Go north on Maple Street and east on Seventh Avenue.
   Ⓒ Go north on Maple Street and east on Sixth Avenue.
   Ⓓ Go south on Beech Street and west on Fifth Avenue.

Stop

Mathematics

PRACTICE 30 • Word Problems

Directions: Solve each problem.

SAMPLES

A. A bus holds 44 passengers. How many buses will be needed to take 430 students and parents on a field trip?

   Ⓐ   5 buses

   Ⓑ   9 buses

   Ⓒ   10 buses

   Ⓓ   11 buses

B. Keesha bought 3 CDs for $14.95 each and one cassette tape for $9.95. There was no sales tax. <u>About</u> how much did she spend in all?

   Ⓐ $45.00

   Ⓑ $55.00

   Ⓒ $65.00

   Ⓓ $75.00

Tips and Reminders

- Figure out what you have to do in each problem and write a number sentence to help you find the answer.

- Draw a picture if it will help you solve the problem.

- If you have trouble solving the problem, try each answer choice to see which one works.

PRACTICE

1. In the western United States, there were 4857 fires in one month in 1994. The year before there were 3635 fires in the same month. How many more fires were there in 1994 than in 1993?

   Ⓐ   8492

   Ⓑ   1722

   Ⓒ   1222

   Ⓓ   1172

2. Four laps around an oval track is 1 mile. If Naomi runs each lap in 2 minutes 20 seconds, how long will it take her to run 1 mile?

   Ⓐ   10 minutes

   Ⓑ   9 minutes 20 seconds

   Ⓒ   8 minutes 40 seconds

   Ⓓ   6 minutes 20 seconds

Go On

3. In 1980, farmers grew 28.0 bushels of soybeans per acre. In 1994, their yield was 40.5 bushels per acre.

Soybeans 28.0/acre 1980   Soybeans 40.5/acre 1994

On 10 acres, how many more bushels of soybeans could a farmer grow in 1994 than in 1980?

- Ⓐ 685 bushels
- Ⓑ 405 bushels
- Ⓒ 280 bushels
- Ⓓ 125 bushels

4. Patrick measured the height of six of his friends. The measurements were 142 cm, 147 cm, 148 cm, 149 cm, 153 cm, and 155 cm. What is their average height?

- Ⓐ 148 cm
- Ⓑ 149 cm
- Ⓒ 150 cm
- Ⓓ 151 cm

5. A student group has $88.00 to spend on fabric to make curtains. They need 30 yards of fabric. <u>About</u> how much can they spend per yard of fabric?

- Ⓐ $2.00 per yard
- Ⓑ $3.00 per yard
- Ⓒ $4.00 per yard
- Ⓓ $5.00 per yard

6. Every day, Alice rides her bicycle 1.7 miles to school, 2.2 miles to the library after school, and 1.8 miles back to her house. <u>About</u> how many miles does she ride each day?

- Ⓐ 12 miles
- Ⓒ 8 miles
- Ⓑ 10 miles
- Ⓓ 6 miles

7. Jon mixes $1\frac{1}{2}$ cups of apple juice, $\frac{3}{4}$ cup of cranberry juice, and $1\frac{1}{2}$ cups of grapefruit juice. How many cups of juice does he make in all?

- Ⓐ $1\frac{3}{4}$ cups
- Ⓑ $2\frac{3}{4}$ cups
- Ⓒ $3\frac{1}{2}$ cups
- Ⓓ $3\frac{3}{4}$ cups

8. The Johnsons spend $1170.00 per year on oil for their home. On average, how much do they spend each month?

- Ⓐ $3.21
- Ⓒ $97.50
- Ⓑ $22.50
- Ⓓ $292.50

9. Millie spent 3 hours doing her homework on Monday, 2 hours 45 minutes on Tuesday, and 2 hours 15 minutes on Wednesday. How much time did she spend in all on her homework in these 3 days?

- Ⓐ 8 hr
- Ⓑ 7 hr 45 min
- Ⓒ 7 hr 15 min
- Ⓓ 7 hr

Go On

10. Eddie bought a 1-gallon jug of liquid soap and poured some into a pint-size container. How many times can he fill the small container from the gallon jug?

   Ⓐ 2
   Ⓑ 4
   Ⓒ 8
   Ⓓ 10

11. There is a bucket full of balls at a miniature golf course. It has 3 green, 5 red, 5 yellow, and 7 blue balls. If you take out one ball without looking, what color are you most likely to get?

   Ⓐ red
   Ⓑ green
   Ⓒ blue
   Ⓓ yellow

12. Mario wrote 2 stories for a total of 10 pages. At this rate, how many pages will he have if he writes 12 stories?

   Ⓐ 24 pages
   Ⓑ 36 pages
   Ⓒ 40 pages
   Ⓓ 60 pages

13. On a map, the distance between two towns is 5 inches. An inch on the map represents 10 miles. What is the actual distance between the towns?

   Ⓐ 0.5 miles
   Ⓑ 5 miles
   Ⓒ 50 miles
   Ⓓ 500 miles

14. There are 6 skeins of yarn in a bag. The bag costs $18.90. What is the cost of each skein of yarn?

   Ⓐ $2.85   Ⓒ $3.00
   Ⓑ $2.95   Ⓓ $3.15

15. Mr. Jenkins's employer allows him 10 holidays during the year. Three of these fall on Mondays, 2 fall on Wednesdays, and 5 fall on Fridays. How many times a year does Mr. Jenkins get to enjoy a 3-day weekend?

   Ⓐ 8 times   Ⓒ 10 times
   Ⓑ 9 times   Ⓓ 13 times

16. Charmayne bought a box of 2 dozen valentines to send to her classmates. She needs 31. How many individual valentines will she need to buy in addition to the box?

   Ⓐ 7   Ⓒ 9
   Ⓑ 8   Ⓓ 10

17. Four students live on the same road. Max lives 2 miles from the school. Claire lives twice as far away as Max. Jim lives between Max and Sue. Sue lives 1 mile from the school. Who lives farthest from the school?

   Ⓐ Max   Ⓒ Jim
   Ⓑ Claire   Ⓓ Sue

18. A movie theater charges $4.50 per ticket. If the theater sells 30 tickets, how much money will be collected?

   Ⓐ $135.00   Ⓒ $13.50
   Ⓑ $125.00   Ⓓ $12.50

Go On →

19. In Albert's class, the ratio of students who prefer soccer to football is 4 to 3. If there are 35 students in the class, how many prefer soccer?

(A) 15   (C) 25

(B) 20   (D) 30

20. Whitney is playing a game with the spinner shown below. If she spins once, what number is she most likely to get?

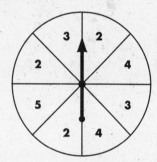

(A) 2   (C) 4

(B) 3   (D) 5

21. Marcos bought 2 pounds of apples and 2 pounds of grapes. How much did he spend in all?

$1.79/lb. $1.05/lb.

(A) $2.10   (C) $5.58

(B) $3.58   (D) $5.68

22. Laura scored 84, 87, 72, 79, and 83 on her science tests. What was Laura's average score?

(A) 80   (C) 82

(B) 81   (D) 83

23. A total of 125 students visited an art museum. They had to stay in groups of 5 students. How many groups of 5 did the students form?

(A) 20   (C) 30

(B) 25   (D) 35

24. A store sold 300 cases of soda in one day. There are 48 cans of soda in a case. <u>About</u> how many cans were sold?

(A) 30,000   (C) 20,000

(B) 25,000   (D) 15,000

25. Mr. Claus drives a delivery truck. The table below shows how many miles he drove each day last week.

Day	Number of Miles
Monday	211
Tuesday	305
Wednesday	288
Thursday	190
Friday	320

<u>About</u> how many miles did he drive in all?

(A) 1200   (C) 1400

(B) 1300   (D) 1500

Stop

Post-test

READING: Vocabulary

Directions: Find the word that means the same, or almost the same, as the underlined word.

1. a <u>blend</u> of juices

   Ⓐ gallon   Ⓒ recipe

   Ⓑ drink   Ⓓ mixture

2. <u>inquire</u> about

   Ⓐ write   Ⓒ ask

   Ⓑ advise   Ⓓ warn

3. a <u>shrewd</u> woman

   Ⓐ tall   Ⓒ polite

   Ⓑ clever   Ⓓ beautiful

4. a <u>fragment</u> of pottery

   Ⓐ piece   Ⓒ treasure

   Ⓑ style   Ⓓ bowl

5. <u>concluded</u> a report

   Ⓐ wrote   Ⓒ shared

   Ⓑ recited   Ⓓ ended

Directions: Find the word that means the OPPOSITE of the underlined word.

6. <u>loosen</u> the ropes

   Ⓐ open

   Ⓑ untie

   Ⓒ tighten

   Ⓓ twist

7. a <u>broad</u> canyon

   Ⓐ narrow

   Ⓑ pretty

   Ⓒ rugged

   Ⓓ wide

Directions: Read the two sentences. Find the word that best fits the meaning of **both** sentences.

8. He leaned his bike against the _____.

Did the coach _____ the names of the players who made the team?

   Ⓐ announce   Ⓒ wall

   Ⓑ post   Ⓓ fence

9. The _____ tire is in the trunk.

Can you _____ a dime?

   Ⓐ extra   Ⓒ lend

   Ⓑ flat   Ⓓ spare

Go On

Directions: Read the sentences. Choose the word that best completes the meaning of each sentence.

Jenny wanted to be a champion gymnast more than anything else in the world. She gave up every other __(10)__ so that she could practice every day. To be a champion, you must __(11)__ long and hard. Any great __(12)__ will tell you the same thing.

10. Ⓐ week
    Ⓑ student
    Ⓒ activity
    Ⓓ habit

11. Ⓐ sleep
    Ⓑ win
    Ⓒ pretend
    Ⓓ train

12. Ⓐ athlete
    Ⓑ professor
    Ⓒ operator
    Ⓓ friend

Directions: Choose the word or phrase that gives the meaning of the underlined prefix or suffix.

13. <u>multi</u>purpose   <u>multi</u>sided
    Ⓐ without
    Ⓑ many
    Ⓒ before
    Ⓓ against

14. <u>inter</u>state   <u>inter</u>personal
    Ⓐ between
    Ⓑ before
    Ⓒ opposed to
    Ⓓ after

15. glori<u>ous</u>   joy<u>ous</u>
    Ⓐ without
    Ⓑ one who
    Ⓒ filled with
    Ⓓ the process of

Directions: Read the sentence and the question. Find the word that best answers the question.

16. The little boy _____ told the officer his name.

    Which word suggests that the boy was shy?

    Ⓐ gently
    Ⓑ timidly
    Ⓒ proudly
    Ⓓ suddenly

17. For Clem, breaking down next to a gas station was _____.

    Which word suggests that Clem was lucky?

    Ⓐ peculiar
    Ⓑ harmless
    Ⓒ dangerous
    Ⓓ fortunate

Stop

Post-test

READING: Comprehension

Directions: Read each passage. Choose the best answer to each question.

Who's afraid of sharks?

People have little reason to fear sharks. More people die every year from bee stings, lightning strikes, and snakebites than from shark attacks. But we fear sharks anyway. They look frightening, and most sharks have large, sharp teeth.

There are more than 350 different kinds of sharks, and they can be found in every part of the world. Unfortunately for them, sharks have become quite valuable. People value sharks mainly for meat, which is now sold in many supermarkets. Shark fins are popular in Asia, and shark hides are used as leather. Other parts of the shark are used in many different products, such as make-up and medicines.

Sharks have no real enemies in the sea and little to fear—except humans. Every year, fishermen catch and destroy between 30 million and 100 million sharks. Scientists believe that at this rate, some kinds of sharks will be extinct within 10 years.

---

18. Fishermen catch sharks mainly as a source of –

(A) medicine
(B) leather
(C) meat
(D) fear

19. A good title for this passage would be –

(A) "Shark-fin Soup"
(B) "Humans' Greatest Fears"
(C) "Sharkskin Shoes"
(D) "Endangered Sharks"

20. This passage is most like a –

(A) myth
(B) biography
(C) mystery
(D) magazine article

21. Which statement is an opinion?

(A) Sharks have no real enemies in the sea.
(B) Sharks look frightening.
(C) Most sharks have sharp teeth.
(D) There are more than 350 different kinds of sharks.

Go On

An Alarming Experience

Miss Maple expected to be delighted at the concert last night, but instead she was mortified. She had taken her seat in the concert hall and was waiting for the music to begin. The players and the conductor had taken their places on stage. As the house lights dimmed, the audience grew absolutely silent. The conductor lifted his arms to begin the music.

Suddenly, there was a loud ringing noise. The conductor turned and stared angrily into the auditorium. The sound seemed to be coming from under Miss Maple's seat, and all eyes were directed at her.

Miss Maple realized with horror that it was the alarm clock she had bought just before the concert. She quickly grabbed the package, jumped up, and ran out the nearest exit with the package ringing all the way. She never returned to hear the music.

---

22. On her way to the concert, Miss Maple stopped to –

Ⓐ eat dinner

Ⓑ buy an alarm clock

Ⓒ listen to some music

Ⓓ take a nap

23. The passage says, "She was mortified." Mortified means –

Ⓐ filled with pleasure

Ⓑ bitter and angry

Ⓒ barely awake

Ⓓ deeply embarrassed

24. "All eyes were directed at her" means that –

Ⓐ everyone stared at her

Ⓑ people yelled at her

Ⓒ she looked at everyone

Ⓓ people moved toward her

25. The author's purpose in this passage is mainly to –

Ⓐ teach a lesson

Ⓑ persuade people to go to concerts more often

Ⓒ tell an entertaining story

Ⓓ describe Miss Maple

26. Who seemed to be most angry?

Ⓐ Miss Maple

Ⓑ the conductor

Ⓒ the players

Ⓓ other members of the audience

What was Arnetta so concerned about?

Arnetta was proud of her new ring—a deep red garnet in a beautiful gold setting. It was a birthday present from her parents, and she could hardly wait to show it off to her friends.

At school, Arnetta talked with her friends before classes began. Several times she acted as if she were brushing her hair out of her eyes, even though it wasn't in her eyes. But nobody noticed the ring.

In class she passed a note to Brenda, her best friend. She kept her hand in the air for a long time after handing the note to Brenda, but Brenda did not notice anything new.

At lunch it was the same story, and Arnetta couldn't bear it any longer. Suddenly she announced, "It's so warm in here, I'll just have to take off MY RING!"

---

27. What happens first in this story?

   Ⓐ Arnetta talks with her friends.

   Ⓑ Arnetta passes a note to Brenda.

   Ⓒ Arnetta receives a birthday present.

   Ⓓ Arnetta joins her friends for lunch.

28. Where does most of this story take place?

   Ⓐ in Arnetta's bedroom

   Ⓑ at Brenda's house

   Ⓒ in a restaurant

   Ⓓ at school

29. Why did Arnetta keep brushing the hair away from her eyes?

   Ⓐ She wanted her friends to see her ring.

   Ⓑ Her hair was bothering her.

   Ⓒ She wanted her friends to see her new haircut.

   Ⓓ It was quite hot in the building.

30. What can you conclude about Arnetta's friends from reading this story?

   Ⓐ They don't like her very much.

   Ⓑ They often compliment her.

   Ⓒ They are not very observant.

   Ⓓ They think she is strange.

31. Which is the best title for this story?

   Ⓐ "Passing Notes"

   Ⓑ "Arnetta's New Ring"

   Ⓒ "The Deep Red Garnet"

   Ⓓ "Marcy's Surprise"

32. How did Arnetta probably feel by the time she got to lunch?

   Ⓐ exasperated

   Ⓑ embarrassed

   Ⓒ discouraged

   Ⓓ suspicious

Go On

The Wrong Joke

Ramon was supposed to go to the dentist, but he didn't want to go. One of his friends had told him terrible things about having his teeth drilled. Ramon's dad tried to calm him down. "It's just for a check-up," Dad said.

"Sure, that's what they told Roberto. Then they practically tortured him to death."

"Ramon, there's no reason to be afraid of the dentist. It's different from when I was your age. These days there's hardly ever any pain."

"Hardly ever isn't never," Ramon grumbled.

In the car, Dad decided to distract Ramon by telling some jokes. "What's the best way to start a fire with two sticks?" he asked.

"Make sure one of them is a matchstick," laughed Ramon.

"I guess you've heard that one," said Dad. "Well, here's another. How is a soldier like a dentist?"

"I don't know," answered Ramon after a long pause.

"They both have to dri–" Dad tried to stop himself, but it was already too late.

"They both have to drill!" shouted Ramon. "Stop the car! I'm not going! Nobody's going to drill my teeth!"

"Oops," groaned Dad. "That was the wrong joke to tell today!"

---

33. What was Ramon's problem?

(A) His dad kept telling the same jokes over and over again.

(B) He felt ill.

(C) He missed his friend Roberto.

(D) He did not want to go to the dentist.

34. What will most likely happen next?

(A) Ramon's dad will take him home.

(B) Dad will tell another joke.

(C) Ramon will go to the dentist.

(D) Ramon will tell a joke.

35. According to Ramon's dad, going to the dentist today is different because –

(A) there is hardly ever any pain

(B) dentists no longer use drills

(C) no one has cavities anymore

(D) no one walks to the dentist's office

36. The theme of this story is mostly concerned with –

(A) comparing soldiers and dentists

(B) fear of the unknown

(C) comparing the old days with today

(D) hope for the future

Stop

Post-test

LANGUAGE ARTS: Mechanics and Usage

Directions: Read each sentence and look at the underlined word or words. Look for a mistake in capitalization, punctuation, or word usage. If you find a mistake, choose the best way to write the underlined part of the sentence. If there is no mistake, fill in the bubble beside answer D, "Correct as is."

1. The Parrot Cafe is the <u>most noisiest</u> restaurant in town.

   Ⓐ most noisy

   Ⓑ noisiest

   Ⓒ most noisier

   Ⓓ Correct as is

2. Gay <u>catched</u> the ball in her glove.

   Ⓐ caughted

   Ⓑ catch

   Ⓒ caught

   Ⓓ Correct as is

3. Minnie said, <u>"Please come over here."</u>

   Ⓐ "Please come over here.

   Ⓑ Please come over here."

   Ⓒ Please come over here.

   Ⓓ Correct as is

4. Isn't that <u>Darnells</u> notebook?

   Ⓐ Darnells'

   Ⓑ Darnell's

   Ⓒ Darnells's

   Ⓓ Correct as is

5. <u>Don't never</u> call me at night.

   Ⓐ Don't ever

   Ⓑ Do not never

   Ⓒ Don't not ever

   Ⓓ Correct as is

6. <u>Mr Julius T Barnes</u> is my boss.

   Ⓐ Mr Julius T. Barnes

   Ⓑ Mr. Julius T. Barnes

   Ⓒ Mr. Julius T Barnes

   Ⓓ Correct as is

7. Will you come with <u>him and I</u>?

   Ⓐ he and I

   Ⓑ he and me

   Ⓒ him and me

   Ⓓ Correct as is

8. I just read a book called *A bridge to terabithia*.

   Ⓐ *A Bridge To Terabithia*

   Ⓑ *A Bridge to Terabithia*

   Ⓒ *a Bridge to Terabithia*

   Ⓓ Correct as is

9. The girls <u>weren't</u> home yet.

   Ⓐ wasn't

   Ⓑ was not

   Ⓒ ain't

   Ⓓ Correct as is

Go On

Directions: Read the sentences and look at the underlined words. Find the underlined word that has a mistake in spelling. If there are no mistakes in spelling, fill in the bubble beside answer D, "No mistake."

10. Ⓐ I will see you <u>tomorow</u>.
    Ⓑ I hope the <u>weather</u> is better.
    Ⓒ Wait just a <u>minute</u>!
    Ⓓ No mistake

11. Ⓐ We will be <u>traveling</u> for two weeks.
    Ⓑ Both <u>famillies</u> will go on the trip.
    Ⓒ It will be a great <u>vacation</u>.
    Ⓓ No mistake

12. Ⓐ Why are you so <u>surprised</u>?
    Ⓑ This is the right <u>address</u>.
    Ⓒ Just <u>remember</u> to ring the bell.
    Ⓓ No mistake

13. Ⓐ She lives in the <u>country</u>.
    Ⓑ Jed <u>preffers</u> life in the city.
    Ⓒ Martha would be happy <u>anywhere</u>.
    Ⓓ No mistake

14. Ⓐ My <u>faverite</u> flavor is vanilla.
    Ⓑ Toni likes <u>chocolate</u> best.
    Ⓒ Kara likes <u>strawberry</u>.
    Ⓓ No mistake

15. Ⓐ Thad is in the <u>hospital</u>.
    Ⓑ We will <u>decorate</u> his room.
    Ⓒ He <u>received</u> many flowers.
    Ⓓ No mistake

Directions: Find the answer that is a complete sentence written correctly.

16. Ⓐ Having lunch at Marcy's.
    Ⓑ The waiter brought the food.
    Ⓒ After the meal, a great dessert.
    Ⓓ Hank and I really enjoyed it we can't wait to go again.

17. Ⓐ A really fancy jack-o'-lantern.
    Ⓑ Resembled a cat's face.
    Ⓒ Gerald knocked it over it smashed.
    Ⓓ I was furious with him.

18. Ⓐ That doesn't seem fair to me.
    Ⓑ It's wrong but it's kind of funny.
    Ⓒ Laughing at the wrong times.
    Ⓓ Mary gets upset so do I.

19. Ⓐ Searching for a new house.
    Ⓑ Something at the right price.
    Ⓒ Mom checks the newspaper.
    Ⓓ Not sure I want to move.

20. Ⓐ We saw a movie it was about a giant octopus.
    Ⓑ Eight very long tentacles.
    Ⓒ It was huge it had beady eyes.
    Ⓓ The movie scared me.

21. Ⓐ Andy rides his rocking horse.
    Ⓑ Pretends that it is real.
    Ⓒ Just a toy made of wood.
    Ⓓ Doesn't want to believe me.

Post-test

LANGUAGE ARTS: Composition

Directions: Read each paragraph. Then answer the questions that follow.

Paragraph 1

It's a stone in the wall of an Irish castle. The castle is located near the town of Blarney. I have visited some castles myself. According to legend, anyone who kisses the Blarney Stone will have the gift of clever speech. Personally, I think that's a lot of "blarney."

---

22. Which is the best topic sentence for this paragraph?

   Ⓐ Do you know about the Blarney Stone?

   Ⓑ Ireland is a country in Europe.

   Ⓒ Have you ever been to Ireland?

   Ⓓ Blarney is a lovely small town.

23. Which is the best way to combine the first two sentences in this paragraph?

   Ⓐ It's a stone in the wall of an Irish castle, and the castle is located near the town of Blarney.

   Ⓑ It's a stone in the wall of an Irish castle the castle is located near the town of Blarney.

   Ⓒ It's a stone in the wall of an Irish castle located near the town of Blarney.

   Ⓓ It's a stone in the wall near the town of Blarney in an Irish castle.

24. Which sentence would fit best at the end of this paragraph?

   Ⓐ There are thousands of stones in Ireland.

   Ⓑ Everyone in Ireland has the gift of clever speech.

   Ⓒ No one has ever been able to reach the Blarney Stone.

   Ⓓ The legend of the Blarney Stone is just another superstition.

25. Which sentence does **not** belong in this paragraph?

   Ⓐ It's a stone in the wall of an Irish castle.

   Ⓑ The castle is located near the town of Blarney.

   Ⓒ I have visited some castles myself.

   Ⓓ According to legend, anyone who kisses the Blarney Stone will have the gift of clever speech.

Go On →

Paragraph 2

Today's actors don't interest me much. Today's actors are more concerned with their looks than with acting. It also seems to me that all the good stories have been done already. Today's movies are just remakes of stories that were written long ago. The only improvement in movies today is the use of special effects.

---

26. Which is the best topic sentence for this paragraph?

Ⓐ I have read that fewer movies are being made today.

Ⓑ I don't think that movies are as good as they used to be.

Ⓒ Movies cost an unbelievable amount of money to make.

Ⓓ Some people would rather watch TV than go out to a movie.

27. Which is the best way to combine the first two sentences in this paragraph?

Ⓐ Today's actors don't interest me much so they are more concerned with their looks than with acting.

Ⓑ Today's actors don't interest me much, who are more concerned with their looks than with acting.

Ⓒ Today's actors don't interest me much, and they are more concerned with their looks than with acting.

Ⓓ Today's actors don't interest me much because they are more concerned with their looks than with acting.

28. Which sentence would best fit at the end of this paragraph?

Ⓐ The special effects have never been better.

Ⓑ My favorite old movie is *To Kill a Mockingbird*.

Ⓒ Cary Grant was a great actor.

Ⓓ The most expensive movie ever made cost more than 120 million dollars.

29. This paragraph was probably written for people who –

Ⓐ make TV shows

Ⓑ are interested in movies

Ⓒ invent special effects

Ⓓ never go to the movie theater

Stop

LANGUAGE ARTS: Study Skills

Directions: Choose the best answer to each question about finding information.

30. If you wanted to find the address of a toy store in your town, you should look in –

Ⓐ an atlas

Ⓑ a magazine

Ⓒ a dictionary

Ⓓ a telephone directory

31. Which name would be listed first in alphabetical order?

Ⓐ Parthenon

Ⓑ Parker

Ⓒ Parnell

Ⓓ Parsons

32. Which of these could be guide words on a dictionary page that includes the word *clone?*

Ⓐ clerical/cling

Ⓑ clinic/clock

Ⓒ cloth/clover

Ⓓ clod/closet

33. In which section of the library would you find encyclopedias?

Ⓐ the fiction section

Ⓑ the reference section

Ⓒ the biography directory

Ⓓ the audiotape section

Use the map to answer question 34.

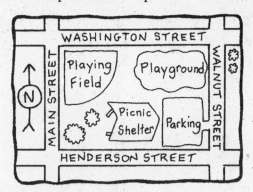

34. The playground is at the corner of which two streets?

Ⓐ Walnut and Henderson

Ⓑ Henderson and Main

Ⓒ Washington and Main

Ⓓ Walnut and Washington

35. In a social studies textbook, where should you look to find the meaning of the word *longitude?*

Ⓐ glossary

Ⓑ table of contents

Ⓒ title page

Ⓓ index

36. To find information in an encyclopedia about Roald Amundsen's trip to the South Pole, you should look under –

Ⓐ Roald

Ⓒ South

Ⓑ Amundsen

Ⓓ Pole

Stop

Post-test

MATHEMATICS: Concepts and Applications

Directions: Choose the best answer to each question.

1. Which numeral shows seventy-one thousand forty-nine?

- Ⓐ 7149
- Ⓑ 70,149
- Ⓒ 71,490
- Ⓓ 71,049

2. What is the value of the **3** in 34,625?

- Ⓐ 3 ten thousands
- Ⓑ 3 thousands
- Ⓒ 3 hundreds
- Ⓓ 3 tens

3. Which numeral has the least value?

- Ⓐ 9108
- Ⓒ 9018
- Ⓑ 9180
- Ⓓ 9810

4. What is 4486 rounded to the nearest hundred?

- Ⓐ 5000
- Ⓒ 4400
- Ⓑ 4500
- Ⓓ 4000

5. Which number comes next in this pattern?

2, 4, 8, 16, 32 __?__ . . .

- Ⓐ 36
- Ⓒ 48
- Ⓑ 40
- Ⓓ 64

6. Which is an odd number?

- Ⓐ 805
- Ⓒ 816
- Ⓑ 820
- Ⓓ 874

7. Which is a factor of 36?

- Ⓐ 5
- Ⓒ 8
- Ⓑ 7
- Ⓓ 9

8. Which is the greatest common factor of 18 and 30?

- Ⓐ 2
- Ⓒ 6
- Ⓑ 3
- Ⓓ 8

9. Which is a multiple of 8?

- Ⓐ 85
- Ⓒ 63
- Ⓑ 74
- Ⓓ 40

10. What fractional part is shaded?

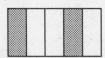

- Ⓐ $\frac{2}{5}$
- Ⓒ $\frac{2}{6}$
- Ⓑ $\frac{2}{3}$
- Ⓓ $\frac{3}{5}$

Go On

11. Which fraction is equivalent to $\frac{6}{10}$?

Ⓐ $\frac{1}{5}$ Ⓒ $\frac{3}{5}$

Ⓑ $\frac{1}{3}$ Ⓓ $\frac{2}{3}$

12. Which fraction is greatest?

Ⓐ $\frac{2}{3}$ Ⓒ $\frac{1}{2}$

Ⓑ $\frac{4}{9}$ Ⓓ $\frac{5}{6}$

13. Which decimal number is equivalent to $\frac{2}{5}$?

Ⓐ 40.0   Ⓒ 0.4

Ⓑ 25.0   Ⓓ 0.25

14. Which decimal number has the greatest value?

Ⓐ 0.061   Ⓒ 6.1

Ⓑ 0.61   Ⓓ 61.0

15. Which number is the arrow pointing to on the number line?

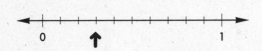

Ⓐ 0.3   Ⓒ 0.5

Ⓑ 0.4   Ⓓ 3.0

16. Which number completes both number sentences?

$45 \div 45 = \square$ $33 \times \square = 33$

Ⓐ 0   Ⓒ 2

Ⓑ 1   Ⓓ 10

17. Choose the missing sign.

$96 \square 6 = 16$

$+$ $-$ $\times$ $\div$

Ⓐ   Ⓑ   Ⓒ   Ⓓ

18. Which point on the grid represents (0, 1)?

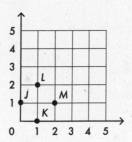

J   K   L   M

Ⓐ   Ⓑ   Ⓒ   Ⓓ

19. Which figure has exactly 4 faces?

Ⓐ   Ⓒ

Ⓑ   Ⓓ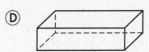

20. What is the diameter of a circle with a radius of 30 cm?

Ⓐ 15 cm   Ⓒ 60 cm

Ⓑ 30 cm   Ⓓ 90 cm

Go On

21. Which is correctly labeled as a line segment?

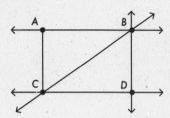

Ⓐ $\overline{AB}$ Ⓒ $\overline{BD}$

Ⓑ $\overline{AC}$ Ⓓ $\overline{CD}$

22. Which figure shows a line of symmetry?

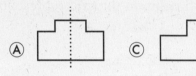

23. What is the volume of this box?

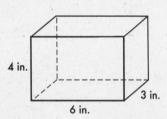

Ⓐ 13 in.³ Ⓒ 48 in.³

Ⓑ 24 in.³ Ⓓ 72 in.³

24. What is the perimeter of this rectangular field?

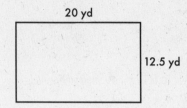

Ⓐ 32.5 yd Ⓒ 65 yd

Ⓑ 40 yd Ⓓ 200 yd

25. Which figure shows an obtuse angle?

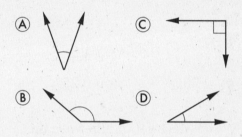

26. What is the area of this square patio?

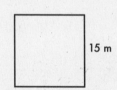

Ⓐ 30 m²

Ⓑ 60 m²

Ⓒ 125 m²

Ⓓ 225 m²

Go On

MATHEMATICS: Concepts and Applications (continued)

Directions: Solve each problem. If the correct answer is Not Given, mark answer D, "NG."

27. Viveca left New Haven by train at 11:05 A.M. She arrived in New York City at 1:20 P.M. How long did the train ride take?

Ⓐ 2 hours 15 minutes

Ⓑ 2 hours 10 minutes

Ⓒ 1 hour 15 minutes

Ⓓ NG

28. Joelle worked 3 days at a craft fair and earned $234.00. Which number sentence should you use to find how much she made on average each day?

Ⓐ 3 + $234.00 = ☐

Ⓑ $234.00 ÷ 3 = ☐

Ⓒ 3 × $234.00 = ☐

Ⓓ $234.00 − 3 = ☐

29. Kenny made 3 pot holders in 2 hours. At this rate, how many pot holders will he make in 10 hours?

Ⓐ 12   Ⓒ 21

Ⓑ 18   Ⓓ NG

30. Tina bought 12 keys for $0.65 each. What else do you need to know to find how much change she should get?

Ⓐ where she bought the keys

Ⓑ how much money she had in all

Ⓒ how much money she gave the clerk

Ⓓ what the keys were for

31. Mia put 310 jellybeans in 6 jars as equally as possible. <u>About</u> how many did she put in each jar?

Ⓐ 50   Ⓒ 70

Ⓑ 60   Ⓓ 80

32. Over 3 days, Cody walked 2.5 km, 3.1 km, and 4.4 km. How far did he walk in all?

Ⓐ 5.6 km   Ⓒ 7.5 km

Ⓑ 6.9 km   Ⓓ NG

Use this graph of Reynaldo's test scores to answer questions 33–34.

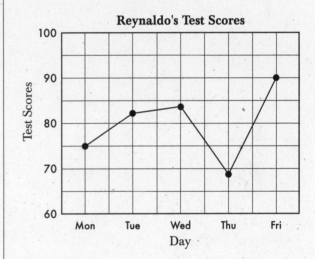

33. What was Reynaldo's highest score?

Ⓐ 69   Ⓒ 90

Ⓑ 84   Ⓓ 100

34. What was his average score?

Ⓐ 75   Ⓒ 82

Ⓑ 80   Ⓓ 85

Stop

Post-test

MATHEMATICS: Computation

Directions: Find the answer to each problem. If the answer is Not Given, choose answer D, "NG."

35. $\frac{3}{8} + \frac{3}{8} =$

   (A) $\frac{5}{8}$

   (B) $\frac{2}{3}$

   (C) $\frac{3}{4}$

   (D) NG

36. $67.46
   $- 34.85$

   (A) \$102.31

   (B) \$91.21

   (C) \$32.61

   (D) NG

37. $325
   \times 6$

   (A) 1820

   (B) 1850

   (C) 2050

   (D) NG

38. \$495.52
   $+ 283.78$

   (A) \$678.20

   (B) \$778.30

   (C) \$779.30

   (D) NG

39. $\frac{5}{6} - \frac{1}{3} =$

   (A) $\frac{1}{2}$

   (B) $\frac{6}{9}$

   (C) $1\frac{1}{6}$

   (D) NG

40. $11\overline{)231}$

   (A) 20

   (B) 21

   (C) 23

   (D) NG

41. $902 + 318 =$

   (A) 1210

   (B) 1220

   (C) 1320

   (D) NG

42. $15 \times 32 =$

   (A) 380

   (B) 460

   (C) 470

   (D) NG

43. $619 \div 18 =$

   (A) 34

   (B) 34 R5

   (C) 34 R7

   (D) NG

44. $4138
   $- 292$

   (A) 3846

   (B) 3946

   (C) 4430

   (D) NG

45. $8.49 \times 7 =$

   (A) \$56.43

   (B) \$58.83

   (C) \$59.43

   (D) NG

Stop

Scoring Chart

Name _____ Class _____

Directions: Use this page to keep a record of your work. Make a check mark (✔) beside each test you finish. Then write your test score.

✔ PRETEST	Score	%
Reading	/36	
Language Arts	/36	
Mathematics	/45	
Total	/117	

✔ POST-TEST	Score	%
Reading	/36	
Language Arts	/36	
Mathematics	/45	
Total	/117	

✔ PRACTICE TEST	Score	%
1. Synonyms/Antonyms	/22	
2. Using Verbs	/12	
3. Whole Number Concepts	/12	
4. Context Clues	/16	
5. Grammar and Usage	/12	
6. Fractions/Decimals	/12	
7. Word Analysis	/8	
8. Sentences	/12	
9. Number Operations	/12	
10. Interpreting Text	/8	
11. Punctuation	/10	
12. Geometry	/15	
13. Main Idea/Details	/12	
14. Capitalization	/10	
15. Measurement	/16	

✔ PRACTICE TEST	Score	%
16. Text Structure	/12	
17. Spelling	/15	
18. Computation	/26	
19. Inferences	/16	
20. Combining Sentences	/10	
21. Estimation	/12	
22. Literary Elements	/12	
23. Composition	/16	
24. Interpreting Data	/20	
25. Evaluating Information	/10	
26. Study Skills	/20	
27. Solving Problems	/16	
28. Making Judgments	/12	
29. Reference Materials	/18	
30. Word Problems	/25	